CSS

MIKE McGRATH

BARNES & NOBLE BOOKS
NEW YORK

In easy steps is an imprint of Computer Step
Southfield Road · Southam
Warwickshire CV47 0FB · United Kingdom
www.ineasysteps.com

This edition published for Barnes & Noble Books, New York
FOR SALE IN THE USA ONLY
www.bn.com

Notice of Liability
Every effort has been made to ensure that this book contains accurate and
current information. However, Computer Step and the author shall not be
liable for any loss or damage suffered by readers as a result of any information
contained herein.

Trademarks
All trademarks are acknowledged as belonging to their respective companies.

Printed and bound in the United Kingdom

ISBN 0-7607-7859-0

Table of Contents

Conventions in this book

CSS keywords (those words that have special meaning in the Cascading Style Sheet specification) and other parts of CSS that appear in the body text are highlighted like this:

... keyword red represents the hexadecimal value #FF0000

Sample code appears in a different font to the regular body text.

CSS code samples:

The CSS style rules appear in bold font, comments appear in normal weight, properties and values are highlighted, like this:

```
/* color h2 headings - red text on yellow background */

h2     { color: red; background: yellow }
```

HTML code samples:

The HTML opening element name, or attribute, targeted by a CSS style rule appears in bold font, and all HTML elements, comments and attributes are colored, like this:

```
<!-- an h2 element targeted by the style rule above -->

<h2>This heading to be styled red on yellow by CSS</h2>
```

The source of each code sample is identified by a file name below the icon that appears alongside the code, like this:

class-selectors.css

class-selectors.html

It should be noted that the listed sample does not necessarily reproduce the entire contents of the named file – only those parts relevant to the example under discussion.

For the convenience of readers, all the CSS sample files listed in this book can be downloaded from this book's page on the publisher's website at http://www.ineasysteps.com.

Introducing CSS

Welcome to the exciting world of Cascading Style Sheets (CSS) – providing greater control over web content than ever before.

This chapter describes the evolution of web page development and shows how style sheets are used with HTML documents. It demonstrates how to create internal style sheets, how to link and import external style sheets, and how to assign inline styles. It also illustrates how the way a browser reads a document can affect how style rules can be overridden.

Covers

Chapter One

Web page evolution

The familiar HyperText Markup Language (HTML) was devised way back in the 1980s by web founder Tim Berners-Lee. It used a number of abbreviations called "tags" to define structural elements of a document such as headings, paragraphs, hyperlinks and lists. The language was not concerned, however, with how the various elements of the document should be displayed.

A major development to HTML arrived in 1993 when college student Marc Andreessen added an <img> tag allowing documents to contain images alongside text. Suddenly documents, with both text and images, became much more visually appealing. This innovation created huge interest in the Internet and websites began to flourish – it was free and anyone could now create exciting web pages with just a plain text editor.

Recognition of the <img> tag was added to the Mosaic web browser – upon which Microsoft Internet Explorer is based. Marc went on to establish the Netscape browser.

As the web grew, its content authors began to demand ways to determine how different elements of their web pages should appear, such as bold and italic text. To satisfy these demands <b> and <i> tags were added to HTML introducing presentational markup to a language previously concerned only with structure. Content authors continued to demand more control so further tags were added providing the ability to color and size text, specify background colors, and even make text "blink" on and off.

The proliferation of presentational HTML tags allowed the creation of rich web page content, but at the expense of document efficiency. Viewing the source code of these web pages often revealed an astonishingly large amount of markup to determine how a relatively small amount of content should appear. For example, an author might markup the title of a document section to control its font, color, and size like this:

```
<font size="+3" face="Arial" color="red">Title</font>
```

Given that this document could have very many section headings, each containing presentational markup, it soon becomes apparent how an abundance of presentational markup tags can easily overwhelm a document. Furthermore, the presentational <font> tag provides no structural indication that this is a section heading.

Recognizing that the mixture of structural and presentational HTML tags was unsatisfactory an alternative solution was sought.

The **CSS** solution

For more on HTML background and utilization please refer to the "HTML in easy steps" title.

The World Wide Web Consortium (W3C) standards body offered a solution to regain control of document markup by separating the structural and presentational aspects. HTML tags continued to define the structural elements of a document, such as headings and paragraphs, but appearance is now defined by rules declared in a "style sheet". A single rule can define the appearance of one or multiple elements "cascading" through the document. This solution is the Cascading Style Sheets (CSS) specification described, by example, throughout this book.

Advantages of CSS presentation

Besides cleanly distinguishing the structural and presentational aspects of a document, CSS brings additional benefits:

- Greater styling possibilities than HTML – allowing you to specify text color and background color, create surrounding borders, increase or decrease surrounding space, set text capitalization and decoration (underlining, etc), even control the element's visibility

- Easier to use than HTML - allowing you to set or modify the appearance of multiple elements with just one rule, rather than requiring the tedious modification of individual HTML elements

- Wider flexibility than HTML – allowing you to create a set of rules in a single centralized style sheet that can be deployed across multiple web pages to provide a consistent website feel

- Smarter than HTML – allowing you to easily provide special styles that intelligently override general style presentation

- More powerful than HTML – allowing you to also control the appearance of certain parts of the interface, such as the cursor

- Better practicality than HTML – allowing you to produce web pages of smaller file size, which download faster.

- Ready for the future – XML may replace HTML as the "lingua franca" of the web and CSS can readily style XML elements.

Creating an internal style sheet

When starting out with CSS it's useful to consider how a document that styles content with HTML presentational tags can be converted to do the same job with CSS style rules.

The HTML code snippet below is taken from the body section of a simple document that displays headings of different sizes. The headings' colors are determined by the value assigned to the color attribute of a nested <font> tag in each case:

html-style.html

```
<!-- headings colors set by font color attribute -->
<h1> <font color = "red"  >h1 Heading</font> </h1>
<h2> <font color = "green">h2 Heading</font> </h2>
<h3> <font color = "blue" >h3 Heading</font> </h3>
<h2> <font color = "green">h2 Heading</font> </h2>
<h1> <font color = "red"  >h1 Heading</font> </h1>
```

To change the color of all <h1> headings in this example you would need to edit the value assigned to the color attribute in the <font> tag nested in both <h1> elements.

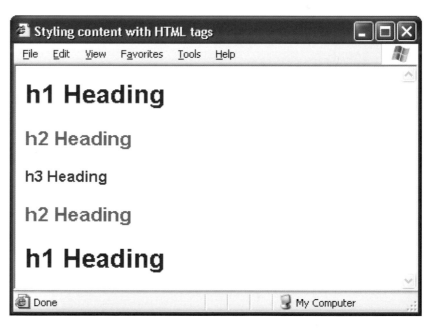

In converting this document to style content with CSS rules all the <font> tags can be removed because they will no longer be needed to set the heading colors – this instantly cleans up the HTML code, leaving only structural tags:

css-style.html

```
<!-- headings colors to be set by style rules -->
<h1>h1 Heading</h1>
<h2>h2 Heading</h2>
<h3>h3 Heading</h3>
<h2>h2 Heading</h2>
<h1>h1 Heading</h1>
```

The style rules can then be added to the head section of the document using HTML <style> tags, declaring the style sheet type as "text/css". The rules in the style sheet listed below specify a color for each of the heading sizes in the document's body section:

css-style.html

```
<!-- internal style sheet for headings colors -->

<style type = "text/css">

h1 { color: red    }

h2 { color: green }

h3 { color: blue   }

</style>
```

To change the color of all <h1> headings in this example you would just need to edit the value assigned to the color property in the h1 style rule.

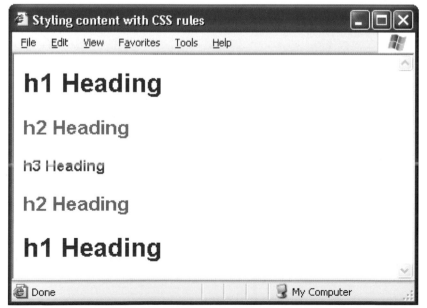

Linking external style sheets

Style sheets which list style rules between <style> tags directly within an HTML document, like the example on the previous page, are known as "internal style sheets" – the style sheet is contained <u>inside</u> the HTML document.

Style sheets may alternatively list style rules in a separate file that is used by the HTML document and, perhaps unsurprisingly, these are known as "external style sheets" – the style sheet exists <u>outside</u> the HTML document.

The <link> tag may only be placed in the head section of an HTML document – not in the body section.

An external style sheet is simply a plain text file with a ".css" file extension. An HTML document can associate an external style sheet by including a <link> tag in its head section to specify the style sheet's relationship, title, type and location, like this:

```
<link rel = "stylesheet" title = "Mikes Styles"
        type = "text/css" href = "link-style.css" >
```

```
<!-- heading color set by style rule -->
<h1>Paragraph Heading</h1>

<!-- paragraph text color set by style rule -->
<p>This paragraph is presented by <span>CSS</span>
style rules.</p>
```

link-style.html

```
h1     { color: blue  }

p      { color: green }

span { color: red    }
```

link-style.css

Notice that the CSS style sheet file just contains a list of style rules – no <style> tags, or any other HTML tags, are required. Single-line and multi-line comments can be added to this file using the C/C++ comment syntax of /* ... */, like the example below:

```
h1    { color: blue  }    /* set all h1 headings blue */

p     { color: green }    /* set general text contained
                             within paragraphs to green */
```

Further <link> elements can be added to the head section of an HTML document to associate alternate style sheets. There must be only one default style sheet relationship so all others must assign the value "alternate stylesheet" to the rel attribute, like this:

```
<link rel = "alternate stylesheet" title = "Big Text"
      type = "text/css" href = "link-style-big.css"  >
```

In browsers that support alternate style sheets their title attribute values are added to the browser menu so the user may choose which to apply to that HTML document, as seen here in Firefox:

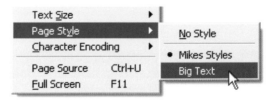

It is especially useful to offer larger size text styles to assist those users with visual impairment.

External style sheets can be linked to multiple HTML documents for consistency and ease of maintenance.

In this example the alternate style sheet improves clarity by using only black-on-white colors and increasing the paragraph text size:

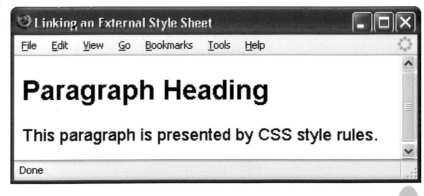

Importing external style sheets

Multiple external style sheets can be associated with an HTML document using @import directives to specify their url location. These must be placed before any other rules in the style sheet and each directive must be terminated by a semi-colon character.

The internal style sheet in the following example uses 3 @import directives to import 3 external style sheets for heading styles before internally declaring a paragraph style rule.

Notice that the entire contents of this internal style sheet are enclosed by HTML <!-- --> comment delimiters – this is considered good practice to have older browsers, which do not support the <style> tag, ignore the contents of the style sheet.

import-style.html

```
<style type = "text/css">
<!--
@import url(import-style-1.css);
@import url(import-style-2.css);
@import url(import-style-3.css);
p { color: purple }
-->
</style>
```

An external CSS style sheet could also begin with @import directives – importing style rules from other external style sheets.

Importing Multiple External Style Sheets

File   Edit   View   Favorites   Tools   Help

h1 Heading color set by imported style sheet #1

h2 Heading color set by imported style sheet #2

h3 Heading color set by imported style sheet #3

This paragraph is presented by CSS style rules.

Done   My Computer

Assigning inline style rules

Style rules can be assigned to the style attribute of any HTML tag which may legally appear in the body section of a document. This "inline" form of style declaration can be found in the source code of many web pages because it is a quick'n'easy way to style a short piece of content. It is, however, best avoided as it contradicts the aim of separating style from content, and it does not offer the advantages provided by centralized style sheets. Furthermore, the style attribute may well not feature in future web standards.

The example below, demonstrating inline style rules, is included here for completeness:

inline-style.html

```html
<h2 style = "color: orange">
Heading color set by inline style</h2>

<p style = "color: fuchsia">
This paragraph is presented by inline style rule.</p>

<ul>
<li style = "color: red">
List Item #1 color set by inline style
<li style = "color: green">
List Item #2 color set by inline style
<li style = "color: blue">
List Item #3 color set by inline style
</ul>
```

Multiple style rules can be assigned within the quotes if each rule is separated from the next by a semi-colon character – more on multiple rule declarations ahead in chapter 2.

Overriding style rules

The previous examples have illustrated the four ways that CSS style rules can be applied to an HTML document – from an internal style sheet, from a linked external style sheet, from an imported external style sheet, and by assignment to the style attribute of an HTML content tag.

More details on how CSS determines style rule status ahead in chapter 3.

It is possible for a single HTML document to collectively employ all these techniques, to determine how its content should appear, but it is worth noting that the order in which the browser reads the style rules can often decide which rule it applies. Where more than one rule of equal status is declared for a particular element the last rule read by the browser will be applied to that element.

In the example below, using all four techniques, the browser first reads the linked style sheet, then the imported style sheet, followed by the internal style sheet, then the assigned style rule. See in the screenshot (opposite top) that, in each case, the last read style rule is the one which has been applied.

override.html (head snippet)

```html
<!-- linked style rules for h1, h2, h3, h4 (red) -->
<link rel = "stylesheet" type = "text/css"
      href = "override-link.css">

<style type = "text/css">

<!-- imported style rules for h1, h2, h3 (green) -->
@import url(override-import.css);

<!-- internal style rules for h1,h2 headings (blue) -->
h1      { color: blue }
h2      { color: blue }

</style>
```

override.html (body snippet)

```html
<!-- assigned style rule for h1 heading (purple) -->
<h1 style = "color: purple">h1 Heading</h1>

<h2>h2 Heading</h2>

<h3>h3 Heading</h3>

<h4>h4 Heading</h4>
```

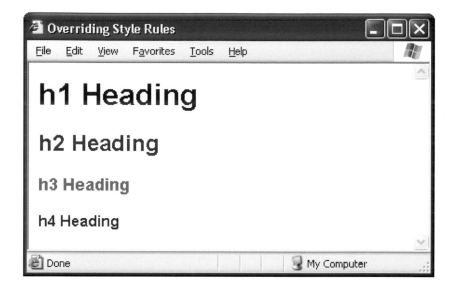

The browser reads the source code sequentially, from start to finish. Therefore, in this case, it reads the rules in the order of (1) linked, (2) imported, (3) internal, (4) assigned.

This means that:

(4)   the assigned rule for the h1 element overrides its internal, imported, and linked rules.

(3)   the internal rule for the h2 element overrides its imported and linked rules.

(2)   the imported rule for the h3 element overrides its linked rule.

(1)   the linked rule for the h4 element is not overridden.

Form the habit of always placing <link> elements before <style> in the HTML document head to avoid confusion.

Re-positioning the <link> element in this example to immediately follow the <style> element has a dramatic effect on how the content is displayed – only the h1 element is then overridden by the assigned rule so all the other headings appear in red, as specified by the rules in the linked style sheet.

Summary

- The HyperText Markup Language (HTML) was created to define document structural elements, such as headings and paragraphs

- Presentational tags, such as <b> and <i>, were added to HTML in response to demand from content authors

- The mixture of structural and presentational markup became unwieldy and is unsatisfactory for future web development

- Cascading Style Sheets (CSS) provides a solution by separating the structural and presentational aspects of HTML documents

- CSS also brings additional benefits of greater styling possibilities, ease of use, wider flexibility and increased practicality

- An internal style sheet can be embedded into an HTML document's head section using <style> tags

- An external CSS style sheet is simply a plain text file, with a ".css" extension, listing one or more style rules

- An external style sheet can be associated with an HTML document using <link> tags in the document's head section

- Additional <link> elements may be added there to associate alternate style sheets which the user can elect to use

- External style sheets can be linked to multiple HTML documents for consistency and ease of maintenance across a website

- One or more external style sheets can be imported into an existing internal or external style sheet using @import directives

- Styles can be assigned "inline" to the style attribute of any HTML tag that is allowed in the body of a document

- Where more than one rule, of equal status, exists for a given element the browser will apply the rule it reads last

Selecting target elements

This chapter describes the structure of style rules in CSS and illustrates, by example, the various ways in which a rule may select elements of an HTML document for styling.

Covers

Chapter Two

Understanding rule structure

In CSS each style rule is comprised of these two main parts:

1. The Selector – specifying which component/s of the HTML document are the target of that rule

2. The Declaration Block – specifying how properties of the target component/s should be styled

A rule begins with the Selector followed by the Declaration Block within a pair of curly brackets (braces). The braces contain one, or more, declarations that each specify a CSS property and a valid value for that property, like in this example:

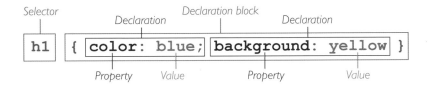

Typically, the Selector targets an HTML element – in this example it targets all the h1 elements within the document for styling.

The Declaration Block in this example contains two declarations to determine the foreground and background colors of the target elements. The CSS color property is assigned a blue value – so each h1 element will have a blue foreground. Similarly, the CSS background property is assigned a yellow value – so each h1 element will have a yellow background.

In conformance with the CSS Specifications the examples listed throughout this book do not add a semi-colon terminator after the final declaration in a declaration block.

Notice how the CSS rule structure uses a colon character to assign a value to a property. Also note that it requires the declarations to be separated with a semi-colon character.

The final declaration in a Declaration Block does not need to be terminated with a semi-colon. However, some web page authors prefer to habitually terminate all CSS declarations so they need not remember to add a separating semi-colon when adding further declarations to an existing rule.

Selecting targets to style

The element selector in a style rule can specify a single target to be styled or it may specify multiple targets as a comma-separated list.

In the style sheet below, a simple CSS rule targets each p paragraph element of the HTML document while another rule targets both h1 and h2 heading elements simultaneously:

```
p           { color: red   }

h1, h2      { color: green }
```

multiple-targets.css

Notice that spaces are ignored in CSS so rules can be formatted for best readability.

Applying these style sheet rules to the selected HTML elements colors each h1 and h2 heading green and each paragraph red.

multiple-targets.html

```
<h1>Heading</h1>

<p>This paragraph is styled by a simple CSS rule.</p>

<h2>Heading</h2>

<p>This paragraph is styled by a simple CSS rule.</p>
```

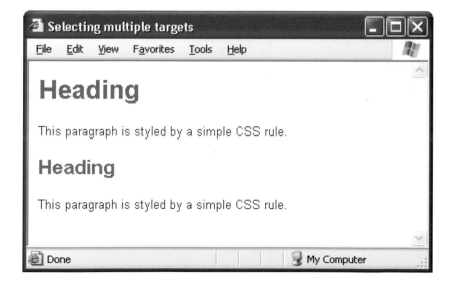

Making multiple style declarations

The Declaration Block in a CSS style rule can contain a single declaration or multiple declarations as a semicolon-separated list.

The style sheet below builds on the previous example by adding a second declaration in each Declaration Block to style foreground and background colors simultaneously:

```
p          { color: red;   background: yellow }

h1, h2     { color: green; background: orange }
```

multiple-styles.css

Notice that a terminating semi-colon has been inserted after each initial declaration – before each second declaration can begin.

Applying these style sheet rules to the selected HTML elements colors each h1 and h2 heading green over an orange background and each paragraph red over a yellow background.

```
<h1>Heading</h1>

<p>This paragraph is styled by a simple CSS rule.</p>

<h2>Heading</h2>

<p>This paragraph is styled by a simple CSS rule.</p>
```

multiple-styles.html

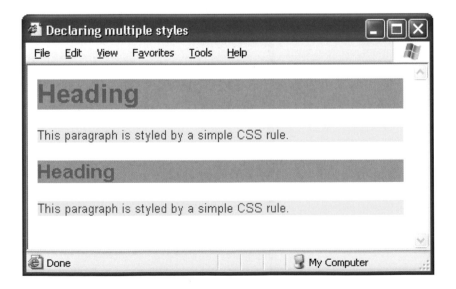

Using the wildcard

The CSS wildcard Selector (a.k.a "universal selector") uses the ★ (asterisk) character to target all elements in an HTML document – like a selector that lists every element in a comma-separated list. This special selector is used in the following style sheet to create a rule setting the foreground color to red for all elements:

```
h1      { background: aqua }

p       { background: yellow }

ul      { background: lime }

*       { color: red }
```

universal-selector.css

universal-selector.html

```
<!-- Paragraph heading -->
<h1>Heading</h1>

<!-- Paragraph text content -->
<p>This paragraph is presented by CSS style.</p>

<!-- Unordered list -->
<ul>
<li>Item 1
<li>Item 2
<li>Item 3
</ul>
```

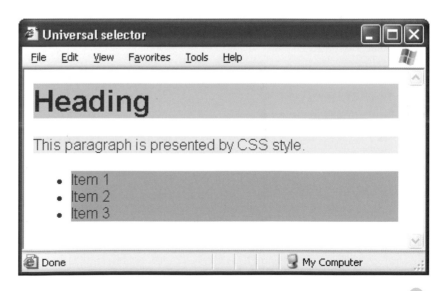

Targeting by class

As an alternative to wholesale selection of HTML document elements a style rule can target a named value that has been assigned to the class attribute of elements. The CSS class selector begins with a period character (.) followed by the name of the target class. This is particularly useful to apply common styling across a range of HTML elements.

Class selectors can be made to target specific elements that have that named class value by adding the element name at the start of the selector. In the following example the Selector targets only the HTML span elements of the named classes – not the p element.

class-selectors.css

```
span.hilite { background: fuchsia }

span.lolite { background: lime     }
```

class-selectors.html

```
<p class = "hilite">You can fool
<span class = "hilite">all</span> the people
<span class = "lolite">some</span> of the time,
<br><span class = "nostyle">and</span>
<span class = "lolite">some</span> of the people
<span class = "hilite">all</span> the time,
<br>but you cannot fool
<span class = "hilite">all</span> the people
<span class = "hilite">all</span> of the time.</p>
```

Change this class selector to simply .hilite to target all elements having that class name.

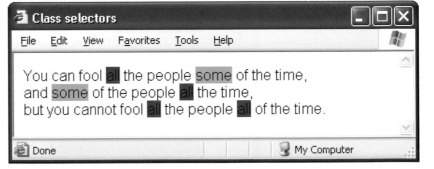

Targeting by identity

In a similar manner to class selection a style rule can target a named value that has been assigned to the id attribute of elements. The CSS identity selector begins with a hash character (#) followed by the name of the target id. This is particularly useful to apply explicit styling to individual HTML elements.

Unlike the class selector an id selector may not specify multiple targets as a comma-separated list – it must only target a single identity attribute. In this example the Selector targets individual HTML elements using the value assigned to their id attribute:

identity-selectors.css

```css
#hd { color: red }
#bf { background: fuchsia }
#eg { background: yellow  }
#st { background: lime    }
#pr { background: aqua    }
#bd { background: orange  }
```

identity-selectors.html

```html
<p><span id = "hd">Top Burger Ingredients:</span>
<br>(Serves 8)</p>
<ul>
<li id = "bf">2 lb ground beef
<li id = "eg">2 eggs
<li id = "st">1 teaspoon salt
<li id = "pr">1 teaspoon black pepper
<li id = "bd">1/2 cup fine bread crumbs </ul>
```

In an HTML document no two id attributes can be assigned the same value – each one should be unique.

Selecting attribute targets

Recall how the class (.) selector and identity (#) selector both target elements to be styled by matching <u>a value</u> assigned to the HTML attributes, class and id respectively.

Additionally CSS can target elements by matching <u>an attribute</u> which the HTML tag contains. For instance, a CSS selector *[src] would target all elements that contain a src attribute within the tag (irrespective of assigned values).

The wildcard universal selector is used to select all elements that make a match.

Furthermore, the selector can specify more than one attribute to target only those elements containing all the specified attributes. For example, a CSS selector *[src][alt] would target all elements that contain both src and alt attributes.

The selector can even seek to match attributes with specific assigned values – a CSS selector *[lang="en"] would target all elements containing a lang attribute with an assigned en value.

Each technique is illustrated in the following example that features an HTML document containing four different a anchor elements:

attribute-targets.html

```
<p><a id = "top">I am an anchor:<br>You cannot click on
me - I have no href attribute.</a></p>

<hr>

<p><a href = "http://www.bn.com">I am a hyperlink to
an external location:<br>Click on me to visit the
destination assigned to my href attribute.</a></p>

<hr>

<p><a href = "http://www.google.com" title = "Click
here for Google search...">I am a hyperlink to an
external location - and I have a tooltip:<br>Click
on me to visit the destination assigned to my href
attribute<br>or hold your mouse pointer over me for
more information.</a></p>

<hr>

<p><a href = "#top">I am a hyperlink to an internal
location:<br>Click on me to go to the anchor at the top
of this page.</a></p>
```

attribute-targets.css

```
/* target all a elements with an href attrib */
a[href]            { color: red }

/* target all a elements with href & title attribs */
a[href][title]     { background: yellow }

/* target all a elements with specific attrib value */
a[href = "#top"]   { background: lime }
```

No style is applied to the a anchor element without an href attribute but all three hyperlinks are set to a red foreground color by the first rule in this style sheet.

The next rule sets a yellow background for links that also contain a title attribute, to which tooltip text can be assigned.

The final rule matches the specific value assigned to a link's href attribute and so sets its background color to be lime.

Attribute targets

File   Edit   View   Favorites   Tools   Help

I am an anchor:
You cannot click on me - I have no href attribute.

I am a hyperlink to an external location:
Click on me to visit the destination assigned to my href attribute.

I am a hyperlink to an external location - and I have a tooltip:
Click on me to visit the destination assigned to my href attribute
or hold your mouse pointer over me for more information.

Click here for Google search...

I am a hyperlink to an internal location:
Click on me to go to the anchor at the top of this page.

http://www.google.com/   My Computer

Selecting partial attribute values

CSS provides two special techniques to select partial attribute values. The first allows the selector to target an element based upon the presence of any single word in an attribute containing a space-separated list of words. Typically this is used to target one of the words assigned to an HTML class attribute.

The syntax to match a single word in an attribute list adds a ~ (tilde) character to the selector, such as *[class ~= "word"].

In the following example the selector matches any HTML class attribute that contains the word "animal" in its assigned value:

all-attrib.css

```
*[class ~= "animal"]        { background: lime }
```

all-attrib.html

```
<p>A list highlighting
<span class = "animal">animal</span> objects:</p>

<ol>
<li class = "reptile">Alligator
<li class = "animal">Race Horse
<li class = "animal" furry">Domestic Cat
<li class = "fish">Barracuda
<li class = "toy animal">Teddy Bear
</ol>
```

*The CSS selector in this example is equivalent to *.animal using dot class notation.*

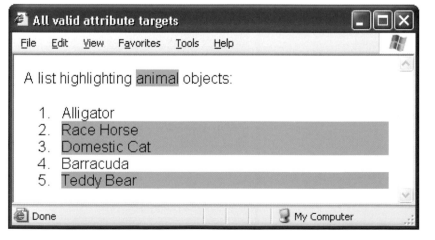

The second special technique that CSS provides to target partial attribute values allows the selector to target an element based upon the beginning of its assigned value, before a hyphen. Typically this is used to target HTML lang attribute values or a series of images.

The hyphen must be included in the image file names to use this technique – ring1.gif, etc. does not work.

The syntax to match the first part of a hyphenated attribute value adds a | (pipe) character to the selector, such as *[lang |= "fr"].

In this example selectors match a series of similarly named images to add background color to their transparent areas and highlight two pieces of Spanish language text:

begin-attrib.css

begin-attrib.html

```css
img[src |= "ring"] { background: fuchsia }
img[src |= "box"]  { background: lime }
img[src |= "tri"]  { background: aqua }
*[lang |= "es"]    { background: yellow; color: red }
```

```html
<p> <img src = "ring-1.gif"> <img src = "box-1.gif">
    <img src = "tri-1.gif">  <img src = "ring-2.gif">
    <img src = "box-2.gif">  <img src = "tri-2.gif">
    <img src = "ring-3.gif"> <img src = "box-3.gif">
    <img src = "tri-3.gif">
</p>
<p lang = "en-us">Hello America</p>
<p lang = "es">Hola España</p>
<p lang = "es-mx">Hola México</p>
```

This example is illustrated with the Firefox web browser – the appearance may vary with Internet Explorer.

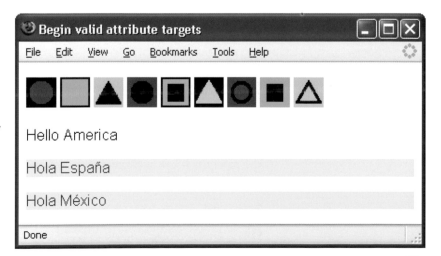

Selecting targets by relationship

CSS can select elements for styling using the HTML document structure. The elements in all HTML documents are arranged in a hierarchical manner descending from the root html element. The next level typically contains the head and body elements. These each contain nested elements which may, in turn, contain further nested elements ...and so on, to complete the hierarchy. The hierarchy of a document could resemble this tree view:

As with people, all elements are a parent, or a child, or in many cases both.

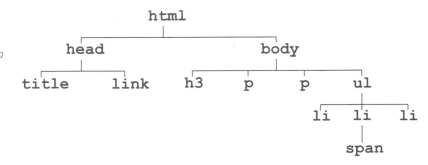

The relationship between a containing element and a nested element on the next hierarchical level is described as "parent-child". So html is the "parent" of the head and body elements, who are themselves "children" of the html element. Similarly the head element is the "parent" of the title and link elements, and the h3, p, and ul elements are all "children" of the body element.

In CSS the selector can target all descendant elements by stating the parent name followed by a space and the child name. For instance, the selector ul.blue li targets all li descendants of an ul element with a class attribute value of "blue".

A selector can target specific child elements by inserting the greater-than > character between the parent and child names. For example, p > span targets all span elements within any p element.

Also a selector may target an adjacent sibling element by inserting the + (plus) character between two specified siblings. For instance, the selector h3 + p targets any p element that immediately follows a h3 element where both have the same parent.

The style rules in the example opposite select descendant, child, and sibling elements from the HTML elements listed.

select-rel.html

```
<body>
<h3>Heading: child</h3>
<p>Paragraph 1: child</p>
<p>Paragraph 2: child <span>Span: grandchild</span></p>

<ul class = "blue">
  <li>List Item 1: grandchild
  <li>List Item 2: grandchild
    <span>Span: great-grandchild</span> </ul>
<ul>
  <li>List Item 1: grandchild
  <li>List Item 2: grandchild
    <span>Span: great-grandchild</span> </ul>
</body>
```

select-rel.css

```
/* select all li descendants of ul.blue element */
ul.blue li { background: aqua }

/* select specific child span elements for li and p */
li > span { background: orange }
p  > span { background: lime }

/* select adjacent p sibling following an h3 element */
h3 + p { background: yellow }
```

The displayed text describes each element's relationship to the <body> element.

Summary

- Each CSS style rule has a Selector and a Declaration Block

- Style rules begin with a Selector specifying one or more target elements to be styled

- The Selector is followed by a Declaration Block specifying one or more declarations within a pair of curly brackets (braces)

- Each declaration assigns a value to an element property using the colon : character

- Multiple declarations in a Declaration Block must be separated from each other using a terminating semicolon ; character

- The wildcard universal selector * can be used in a style rule to target all elements

- A style rule selector can target an element by matching the value assigned to its HTML class attribute using the period . character

- A style rule selector can target an element by matching the value assigned to its HTML id attribute using the hash # character

- Style rule selectors can target elements by exactly matching a value assigned to one or more HTML attributes

- Style rule selectors can target elements by matching partial attribute values that are space-separated or hyphenated

- The elements in all HTML documents are arranged in a hierarchical manner descending from the root html element

- Style rule selectors can use the document structure to target descendant, child and sibling elements

Determining rule status

This chapter describes how the web browser assesses CSS style rules to determine their status in a process called the "Cascade". It illustrates how this evaluation ensures that the rules of highest status are applied where multiple style rules conflict.

Covers

Chapter Three

Performing the cascade

Before a web browser applies CSS style rules to an HTML document it first performs a series of evaluations that it "cascades" down to determine which declarations to apply.

It's important to recognize the sequence of these evaluations in order to understand how the cascade resolves conflicting declarations and determines the final document presentation:

1 Locate declarations – find all declarations that contain a selector matching a given element from inline declarations, internal style sheets, and external style sheets

2 Sort declarations by weight and origin – giving greater weight to any declarations marked as !important and sorting declarations according to whether their origin is user agent (browser), reader (user) or author (style sheet author). For normal weight declarations author origin receive highest status, reader origin receive medium status, and browser origin receive lowest status. But !important reader declarations are allotted higher status than all others, including !important author declarations

3 Sort declarations by specificity – using a given set of criteria to allot higher status to declarations that most specifically target an element

4 Sort declarations by order – allotting higher status to declarations that appear latest in the style sheet or document

The examples that follow in this chapter demonstrate how declarations are sorted by each process in the cascade sequence to determine which rules receive highest status and so get applied to the HTML element.

The browser ends the cascade when it establishes a rule to have clear prominence.

Announcing important rules

A CSS style rule declaration can be given extra weight by adding the flag term !important to the end of the declaration - just before the final brace or terminating semicolon. This designates that rule to be more important than others that target the same element.

The cascade groups important rules together and allocates them higher status than normal declarations. It then proceeds, to resolve conflicts with other important rules that target the same element.

In this example the first two rules that target by id and class override the third rule that targets by element name as they more specifically target the element – i.e. they have greater specificity:

important-rules.css

```
p#line-1     { background: yellow }
p.line-2     { background: orange }
p            { background: aqua   }
```

important-rules.html

```
<p id = "line-1">I am two fools, I know</p>

<p class = "line-2">For loving and for saying so</p>
```

Be sure to insert the !important flag correctly, at the end of a declaration – otherwise it will be ignored.

Here the first paragraph gets a yellow background style and the second paragraph gets an orange background style. Adding an !important flag term to the third rule so it looks like this:

```
p     { background: aqua !important }
```

elevates its status above the others so now this rule is applied and both paragraphs get an aqua blue background style:

```
Announcing important rules
File   Edit   View   Favorites   Tools   Help

I am two fools, I know

For loving and for saying so

Done                                    My Computer
```

Creating browser and user styles

Web browsers have their own intrinsic set of basic style rules to provide a default presentation style for displaying HTML documents – typically black text on a white background in a pre-determined font style and size.

The browser's basic default style rules can often be amended by the user to suit their personal taste. For instance, on the Internet Explorer taskbar click Tools | Internet Options | General | Colors to launch the Colors dialog revealing the default Text and Background color settings. Usually these will be black Text on a white Background – the equivalent of this CSS rule:

```
body  { color: black; background: white }
```

Changing the Text setting to Red in the Colors dialog, as seen below, is the equivalent of changing the browser's style rule to:

```
body  { color: red; background: white }
```

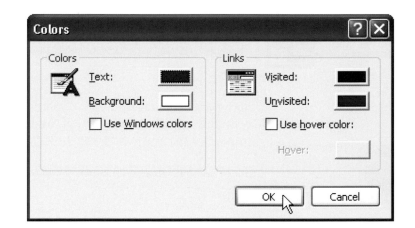

These instructions may relate to a particular browser version – refer to your browser's Help documentation to discover how to amend its default styles.

Click the OK button then restart Internet Explorer to apply the new default setting. Now HTML text content will appear in red on a white background by default. Notice that this procedure amends the <u>Browser</u> styles – it does not create <u>User</u> styles.

The default Browser styles will be applied unless they are overridden by an alternative style in a User-defined style sheet or by an Author-defined style sheet or inline declaration.

Web browsers also allow the User to nominate a style sheet to provide a custom presentation style for displaying HTML documents – typically a list of User-defined rules that reflect their personal preference for colors and fonts. For instance, on the Internet Explorer taskbar click Tools | Internet Options | General | Accessibility to launch the Accessibility dialog. Check the box to "Format documents using my style sheet" then browse to the location of your User-defined style sheet:

Store the User-defined style sheet in the root directory so it's easy to locate when you need to update your personal style preferences.

Click the OK button then restart Internet Explorer to apply the new custom setting. HTML document content will appear in the colors specified in the <u>User</u> style rules created in the nominated style sheet – overriding the default <u>Browser</u> styles.

The default Browser styles will now only be applied if they are not overridden by an alternative User style or by an Author-defined style sheet or inline declaration.

Considering origins and weights

The following example demonstrates how the cascade first sorts CSS declarations by origin and weight, with the Browser styles set to red text on white background – as described on page 36.

The HTML document listed below contains five HTML h2 heading elements to which style rules will be applied:

origins-weights.html

```
<h2>Browser-styled normal heading</h2>
<h2 class = "user">User-styled normal heading</h2>
<h2 class = "author">Author-styled normal heading</h2>
<h2 class = "important-1">
User-styled important heading #1</h2>
<h2 class = "important-2">
User-styled important heading #2</h2>
```

The first h2 element is not targeted by any User or Author rule so the Browser style is applied to color the text red.

The User style sheet, listed first below, has a rule that targets the class attribute value of the second h2 element. This rule has a higher status than the Browser rule and is not overridden by any Author rule so the User style is applied to color the text green.

my-stylesheet.css

```
/* normal weight user origin */
h2.user        { color: green }

/* normal weight user origin - gets overridden */
h2.author      { color: purple }

/* important weight user origin - overrides */
h2.important-1      { color: orange !important }

/* important weight user origin - overrides */
h2.important-2      { color: fuchsia !important }
```

origins-weights.css

```
/* normal weight author origin - overrides */
h2.author      { color: blue }

/* normal weight author origin - gets overridden */
h2.important-1      { color: lime }

/* important weight author origin - gets overriden */
h2.important-2      { color: maroon !important }
```

The User style sheet also has a rule that targets the class value of the third h2 element. But a rule in the Author style sheet has the same target. The Author rule has higher status than both User and Browser rules so the Author style is applied to color the text blue.

Both User and Author rules target the final two h2 elements. Normally the Author rules would be applied but the User declarations each contain an !important flag to elevate their status above that of the Author rules – even when the Author rule itself contains an !important flag. So the important User styles are applied to color the text orange and fuchsia respectively:

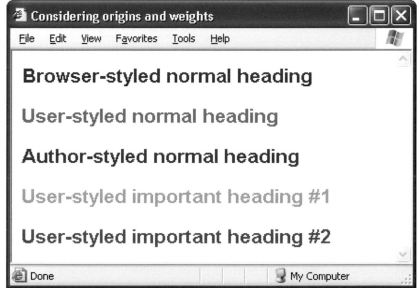

Only Author and User style rules can use the !important flag to add weight – Browser style rules cannot.

So the cascade first sorts style declarations by origin and weight into this order, from highest status to lowest status:

(1) important User declaration

(2) important Author declaration

(3) normal Author declaration

(4) normal User declaration

(5) normal Browser declaration

Calculating selector specificity

Where conflicting declarations remain, after sorting by origin and weight, the cascade examines their selectors to evaluate how specifically each one targets the element. This process awards points for each selector component to calculate a specificity value for each rule. The cascade then uses these to assess the status of each rule – the higher its specificity value, the higher is its status.

A specificity value has four "registers" expressed as a comma-separated list. For instance, a zero specificity value is 0, 0, 0, 0. The actual declaration specificity value is calculated like this:

See the Appendix for full details on pseudo-classes and pseudo-elements.

- for each element and pseudo-element in the selector add 0, 0, 0, 1

- for each class attribute value, attribute selection or pseudo-class in the selector add 0, 0, 1, 0

- for each id attribute value in the selector add 0, 1, 0, 0

- for inline style attribute declarations add 1, 0, 0, 0

The cascade compares specificity values reading from left to right and stopping when it determines that of highest value. For example, 0, 1, 0, 0 is clearly of higher value than 0, 0, 1, 0.

This example illustrates how the cascade allots highest status to the rules with highest specificity value – and only applies those styles.

specificity.html

```
<!-- inline rule specificity = 1,0,0,0 -->
<h2 style = "background: orange">Inline rule style</h2>

<h2 id = "header-1">Identity style</h2>

<h2 class = "headers">Class style</h2>

<h2>Element style</h2>
```

The HTML document has four h2 heading elements to be styled. The first of these includes an inline style declaration – which always have the highest specificity value. The style sheet opposite contains conflicting rules to style the remaining h2 elements. Each has the same origin and weight so the cascade must calculate and compare their specificity values to determine which styles to apply.

specificity.css

```
/* comments denote selector specificity of each rule  */

#header-1           { background: red    } /* 0,1,0,0 */
h2#header-1         { background: maroon } /* 0,1,0,1 */
body h2#header-1    { background: fuchsia} /* 0,1,0,2 */

.headers            { background: green  } /* 0,0,1,0 */
h2.headers          { background: olive  } /* 0,0,1,1 */
body h2.headers     { background: lime   } /* 0,0,1,2 */

h2                  { background: blue   } /* 0,0,0,1 */
body h2             { background: aqua   } /* 0,0,0,2 */
```

The wildcard * universal selector has a zero specificity value of 0, 0, 0, 0.

Calculating selector specificity

File Edit View Favorites Tools Help

Inline rule style

Identity style

Class style

Element style

Done   My Computer

So after first sorting by origin and weight the cascade sorts style declarations by specificity into this order, from highest status to lowest status:

(1) inline declarations

(2) identity declarations, ranked by sum specificity value

(3) class declarations, ranked by sum specificity value

(4) element declarations, ranked by sum specificity value

(5) wildcard declarations, having a zero specificity value

Inheriting styles

In CSS the principle of inheritance allows a single style declaration to be applied to a specified element and automatically to all its descendants. For instance, a rule styling the text color of an unordered list ul element will automatically be applied to its descendant li list elements. It will also be applied to any further descendants, such as the nested ordered list in this illustration:

A tree view of this document helps to clarify how the style rule targeted at the ul element is inherited by all its descendants:

Most "box-model" properties, such as borders and margins, are not automatically inherited as that is generally not the preferred appearance.

The declaration targeting this ul element would have a specificity of 0, 0, 0, 1 but the descendant elements, whilst inheriting the style, have no specificity value whatsoever – not even zero value.

It is important to recognize the distinction between the zero specificity value of a wildcard ★ selector 0, 0, 0, 0 and the absence of specificity value in elements that merely inherit styles as this can produce unexpected consequences. To understand how this effect may appear confusing consider the following example:

inhertiting-styles.html
(body snippet)

```
<h2>what is <span>this</span> problem?</h2>
<ol>
<li>Wildcard selectors have ZERO specificity
<li>Inherited values have NONE
<li>ZERO specificity is higher than NONE
</ol>
```

inhertiting-styles.css

```
/* set all elements text to red */
*       { color: red }

/* set all h2 text to blue */
h2      { color: blue }
```

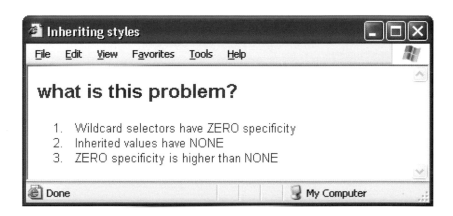

Here the wildcard rule (specificity value 0, 0, 0, 0) sets all element's text to red and a second rule (specificity value 0, 0, 0, 1) sets the h2 heading text to blue.

*Use the wildcard * selector with care, or avoid it entirely, to prevent unexpected results with inherited values.*

Given that the second rule has a higher specificity value than the first rule it might seem reasonable to expect the contents of the span element to inherit the blue color from the h2 element rule. But inherited values have no specificity at all, whereas the wildcard universal selector that targets all elements directly, including these span elements, has a zero specificity. So the wildcard rule has a higher status and the red color is applied to the span contents.

Sorting by order

Where conflicting declarations remain, after sorting by weight and origin, and after sorting by specificity, the cascade allots highest status to the one that it encounters last.

The following example demonstrates how the cascade applies style rules from external and internal style sheets according to order:

sort-order.html
(body snippet)

```html
<h2 id = "hdr-1">Linked style</h2>

<h2 id = "hdr-2">Imported style:
<br>overriding linked style</h2>

<h2 id = "hdr-3">Internal style:
<br>overriding linked and imported styles</h2>

<h2 id = "hdr-4">Internal style: overriding linked,
<br>imported and previous internal styles</h2>
```

The HTML document above contains four h2 heading elements that are targeted by declarations in the external style sheet below:

external-sort-order.css

```css
/* color all headings RED */
#hdr-1 { color: red }
#hdr-2 { color: red }
#hdr-3 { color: red }
#hdr-4 { color: red }
```

Similarly, a second external style sheet contains rules that target the last three h2 heading elements:

import-sort-order.css

```css
/* color last three headings GREEN */
#hdr-2 { color: green }
#hdr-3 { color: green }
#hdr-4 { color: green }
```

In the HTML document head section, shown opposite, a link element first links the rules in the first external style sheet. Next the internal style sheet begins by importing the second external style sheet then makes internal declarations targeting the last two h2 heading elements. The cascade reads these rules in the order of linked, imported, internal, applying the last one in each case.

sort-order.html
(head snippet)

```
<!-- LINK AN EXTERNAL STYLE SHEET -->
<link type = "text/css" rel = "stylesheet"
      href= "external-sort-order.css">

<!-- INTERNAL STYLE SHEET -->
<style type = "text/css">

/* import an external style sheet */
@import url(import-sort-order.css);

/* internal style rules... */
/* color last two headings BLUE */
#hdr-3      { color: blue }
#hdr-4      { color: blue }

/* color last heading ORANGE */
#hdr-4      { color: orange }

</style>
```

If the link element was moved to follow the style element the linked rules would be read after the imported and internal rules – changing the appearance of the headings.

It is considered good practice to place link elements before the style element in the HTML document head.

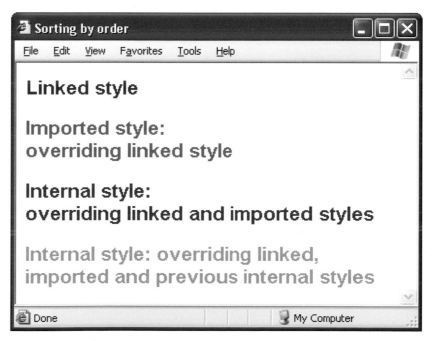

So when everything else is equal the cascade uses the rule order as a sure-fire method to determine the document's appearance.

Summary

- The "Cascade" determines which rule to apply when there are conflicting declarations

- Initially the Cascade locates all style declarations and applies those which do not conflict

- To begin resolving conflicting declarations the Cascade next considers the weight and origin of each declaration

- Rules that contain an !important flag are given greater weight than other "normal" rules

- Normal weight rules are ranked from highest to lowest as author, reader, browser, by origin

- Reader declarations that contain an !important flag out-rank all others

- The Cascade applies those rules resolved by sorting weight and origin then evaluates selector specificity for remaining conflicts

- Specificity values are based upon the number of element, class attribute, and id attribute components in a style sheet rule

- An inline declaration, assigned to the style attribute of an HTML element, has a greater specificity value than all other declarations

- A wildcard selector has a specificity value of zero – but this still overrides inherited values which have no specificity value at all

- The Cascade applies those rules resolved through sorting by specificity then sorts by order to resolve any remaining conflicts

- Those style declarations encountered latest are applied

Describing property values

This chapter explains each type of unit value that can be assigned to a CSS property. Examples demonstrate how these can be used in a variety of ways to define a property's color, quantity, length, location, or state.

Covers

Chapter Four

Painting colors

The examples so far in this book have used some of the 17 color "keywords" that are defined in CSS to represent standard colors. The complete list of standard color keywords are shown below:

red	green	blue
fuchsia	lime	aqua
maroon	olive	navy
orange	yellow	teal	purple
silver	black	white	gray

Web browsers will often recognize many more color names (often up to 140) but these are the standard colors defined in the CSS specifications.

While the standard named colors are convenient to use they provide only a limited choice. Fortunately CSS allows authors to create their own custom colors.

Each color can be defined by the quantity of red, green and blue that needs to be mixed together to form that particular color. For instance, the standard olive color above comprises 50% red, 50% green and 0% blue. This can be expressed in RGB notation form as rgb(50%, 50%, 0%) for assignment to a CSS property like this:

```
h1 { color: rgb(50%, 50%, 0%) } /* color: olive */
```

Specifying different amounts of red, green, and blue, in this way can assign to a property any custom color the author desires.

As an alternative to specifying each color component as a percentage the author may choose an integer value in the range 0-255 for each component. In this format the RGB notation for the standard olive color would look like this:

```
h1 { color: rgb(128, 128, 0)    /* color: olive */
```

A second alternative to specifying each color component as a percentage, or integer value, allows the author to choose a hexadecimal value in the range 00-FF for each component. In this format the standard olive color can be assigned like this:

```
h1 { color: #808000 }           /* color: olive */
```

The table opposite lists the ways in which each standard color can be assigned to a CSS property using these various methods.

Color	Percentage	Integer	Hex
Black	rgb(0%, 0%, 0%)	rgb(0, 0, 0)	#000000
Red	rgb(100%, 0%, 0%)	rgb(255, 0, 0)	#FF0000
Orange	rgb(100%, 65%, 0%)	rgb(255, 165, 0)	#FFA500
Yellow	rgb(100%, 100%, 0%)	rgb(255, 255, 0)	#FFFF00
Fuchsia	rgb(100%, 0%, 100%)	rgb(255, 0, 255)	#FF00FF
Lime	rgb(0%, 100%, 0%)	rgb(0, 255, 0)	#00FF00
Aqua	rgb(0%, 100%, 100%)	rgb(0, 255, 255)	#00FFFF
Blue	rgb(0%, 0%, 100%)	rgb(0, 0, 255)	#0000FF
White	rgb(100%, 100%, 100%)	rgb(255,255,255)	#FFFFFF
Maroon	rgb(50%, 0%, 0%)	rgb(128, 0, 0)	#800000
Olive	rgb(50%, 50%, 0%)	rgb(128, 128, 0)	#808000
Purple	rgb(50%, 0%, 50%)	rgb(128, 0, 128)	#800080
Green	rgb(0%, 50%, 0%)	rgb(0, 128, 0)	#008000
Teal	rgb(0%, 50%, 50%)	rgb(0, 128, 128)	#008080
Navy	rgb(0%, 0%, 50%)	rgb(0, 0, 128)	#000080
Gray	rgb(50%, 50%, 50%)	rgb(128, 128, 128)	#808080
Silver	rgb(75%, 75%, 75%)	rgb(192, 192, 192)	#C0C0C0

Shorthand hex notation can appear confusing – it is described here for completeness but it may be clearer to use standard notation.

Hexadecimal color values comprising three pairs of matching digits can alternatively be expressed using CSS shorthand notation that represents each pair of digits by a single digit. For instance, the hexadecimal value of the standard color red is #FF0000 but can be specified in shorthand as #F00. Similarly black #000000 can be written as #000 and white #FFFFFF as #FFF.

The author is free to choose which color notation method to use according to their preference. Declarations in the style rules below show how each method might be used to specify a custom color:

```
h1    { color: rgb( 85%, 15%, 0%) } /* a custom red    */
h2    { color: rgb( 0, 192, 12) }   /* a custom green */
h3    { color: #042BDF }            /* a custom blue   */
h4    { color: #DE2 }      /* a custom yellow (#DDEE22) */
```

Setting absolute sizes

When assigning any none-zero size value to a CSS property the declaration must include a two-letter unit name to specify which unit of measurement to apply.

The CSS specification provides a range of unit names representing real world units of absolute measurement, as listed in this table:

Zero values can be assigned using just a "0" character – without specifying any unit name.

Unit	Description	Example
in (inches)	American standard unit of length measurement	div { width: 1in }
cm (centimeters)	Metric unit of length where 2.54 centimeters is equivalent to 1 inch	div { height: 2.54cm }
mm (millimeters)	Metric unit of length (one-tenth of one centimeter) where 25.4 millimeters is equivalent to 1 inch	div { height: 25.4mm }
pt (points)	Typographical unit of font height where 72 points is equivalent to 1 inch	div { font-size: 72pt }
pc (picas)	Typographical unit of font height where 6 picas is equivalent to 1 inch	div { font-size: 6pc }

This example introduces the font-size property – one of the CSS font properties detailed in the next chapter.

The style rules in the example opposite use each of these absolute units to set the size of **div** elements, and the height of their text.

In reality the web browser is unlikely to exactly create the absolute dimensions due to differences in monitor size and resolution. For instance, with the first **div** element in this example the browser does not create an on-screen box actually measuring 2 inches by 3 inches - merely its interpretation of those dimensions.

It does, however, use the same interpretation for all absolute units so while the dimensions may not be created accurately they do appear in proportion to each other. More importantly, it maintains the interpreted dimensions irrespective of how the user may re-size the browser window - so absolute dimensions are "fixed".

absolute-sizes.html

```
<div id = "div-1">div-1
<br>2in high x 3in wide</div>

<div id = "div-2">div-2
<br>7.62cm high x 2.54cm wide</div>

<div id = "div-3">div-3
<br>25.4mm high x 76.2mm wide</div>
```

absolute-sizes.css

```
/* set div sizes and font sizes */
#div-1 {        width: 3in;   height: 2in;
                font-size: 0.6in                    }

#div-2 {        width: 2.54cm; height: 7.62cm;
                font-size: 16pt                     }

#div-3 {        width: 76.2mm; height: 25.4mm;
                font-size: 1.75pc                   }
```

The absolute position of these div elements is also controlled by CSS rules – for more details see chapter 9.

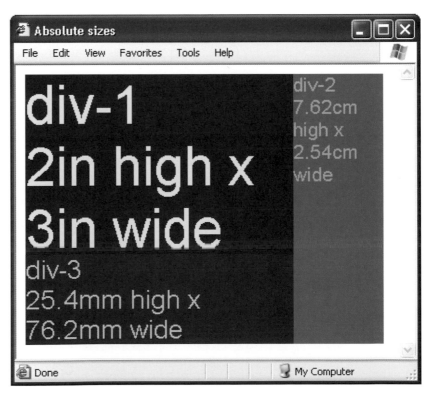

Setting relative sizes

In addition to those units provided to describe absolute values of size (described on the previous page) the CSS specification also provides the units in the table below to describe relative values:

Unit	Description	Example
em (font size)	Abstract typographical unit of font size where 1em is equivalent to the overall height of a given font	div { font-size: 14pt } (1em = 14pt)
ex (font size)	Abstract typographical unit of font size where 1ex is equivalent to the height of lowercase "x" in a given font (often 50% of 1em)	div { font-size: 14pt } (1ex = 7pt)
px (pixels)	Abstract unit representing the dots on a computer monitor where there are 1024 pixels on each line when the monitor resolution is 1024 x 768	div { height: 100px }

A percentage value can also be used to specify a relative size – so assigning a width property a value of 50% makes the target element half the width of its containing element.

Relative units are measured in relation to external items – a given font in the case of em and ex units and monitor settings in the case of px units. Changing the external item they are measured against automatically changes how the relative values appear. For instance, by changing the given font or monitor resolution.

The following example shows how relative values are computed from external absolute values and applied to inner elements:

relative-sizes.css

```
dl          { font-size: 18pt; color: navy }
#line-2     { font-size: 0.9em }
#line-3     { font-size: 0.75em }
#line-4     { font-size: 0.6em }
#credit     { font-size: 1em }

#box-1 { width: 390px; height: 100px; background:lime }
#box-2 { width: 85%; height: 85%; background: aqua     }
#box-3 { width: 85%; height: 85%; background: yellow   }
```

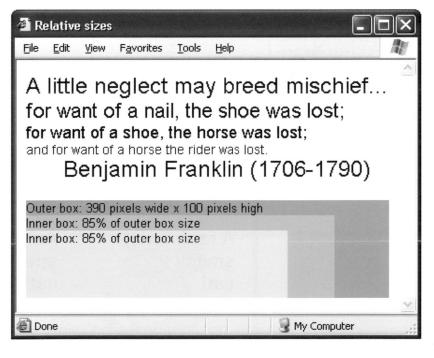

relative-sizes.html

```
<dl>
<dt id = "line-1">
A little neglect may breed mischief...</dt>
<dt id = "line-2">
for want of a nail, the shoe was lost;</dt>
<dt id = "line-3">
for want of a shoe, the horse was lost;</dt>
<dt id = "line-4">
and for want of a horse the rider was lost.</dt>
<dd id = "credit">Benjamin Franklin (1706-1790)</dd>
</dl>

<div id = "box-1">
Outer box: 390 pixels wide x 100 pixels high
<div id = "box-2">Inner box: 85% of outer box size
<div id = "box-3">Inner box: 85% of outer box size
</div>  </div>  </div>
```

Notice how the relative size is computed from each parent element. Specify absolute size for parent elements and relative size for descendants to allow all elements to be re-sized proportionately just by changing the parent's size value.

Addressing locations

A CSS property can be assigned a file resource value by specifying its url location – in the same way that an @import directive is assigned an external style sheet for import into a document. In each case the location may be specified as either a relative address, for resources local to the CSS style sheet's location, or as an absolute address, for resources in remote locations. For instance, addressing a local image file with url(images/my-picture.png) or a remote file with url(http://my-server/images/my-picture.png).

The following example simply assigns a local image resource to the background property of two HTML div element by specifying its location relative to the style sheet below:

locations.css

```
div { width: 150px;
      height: 150px;
      color:red;
      background: url(images/smiley-cat.png) }
```

locations.html

```
<div>
<h2>A real<br>smiley<br>cat!</h2>
</div>

<div>
<h2>Another<br>smiley<br>cat!</h2>
</div>
```

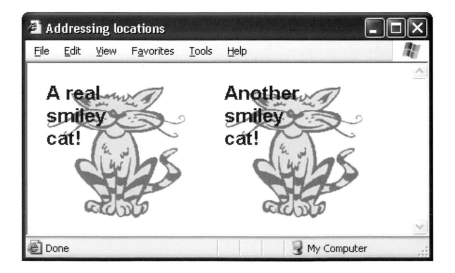

Using keywords

CSS provides a number of "keywords" that can be used to assign values to CSS properties. These are words of special significance that represent intrinsically recognized values. For instance, each of the standard color names is a CSS keyword, representing a known color value - the keyword black represents the hex value #000000.

Keywords are introduced through this book as each CSS property is explored in turn.

The none and inherit keywords can be applied to many properties. The none keyword represents a null value and can be used to explicitly force a value to be removed. Similarly the inherit keyword can force an element to inherit a value from its parent.

The none and inherit keywords are used in the example below to force the default underline text-decoration to be removed from hyperlinks and to force the links to inherit the color value of its parent - overriding the browser's default styles in each case.

keywords.css

```
h3              { color: red; background: yellow }

#menu-2 a       { text-decoration: none; color: inherit }
```

keywords.html

```
<h3 id = "menu-1">Menu:
<a href = "a.html">Link 1</a> |
<a href = "http://w3c.org">Link 2</a>  |
<a href = "z.html">Link 3</a></h3>

<h3 id = "menu-2">Menu:
<a href = "a.html">Link 1</a> |
<a href = "http://w3c.org">Link 2</a>  |
<a href = "z.html">Link 3</a></h3>
```

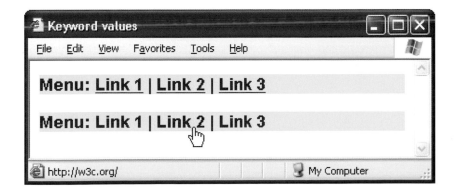

Summary

- The CSS specifications defines names for 17 standard colors

- Each standard color name is a CSS "keyword" value that can be assigned to a CSS property

- Color values can be expressed using RGB notation

- The amounts of red, green, and blue components in RGB notation can be specified as percentages or numerically in the range 0-255

- Color values can be expressed in hexadecimal form as #RRGGBB

- None-zero absolute size values must include a two-letter unit name to denote the unit of measurement (in, cm, mm, pt, or pc)

- None-zero relative size values must also include a two-letter unit name to denote their unit of measurement (em, ex, px)

- Zero absolute or relative values need not include any unit name

- A CSS property can be assigned a file value by stating its absolute or relative address within the parentheses of a url() statement

- CSS "keywords" are words of special significance that represent recognized values (eg. keyword black represents hex #000000)

- The none keyword represents a null value and can be used to explicitly force a value to be removed

- The inherit keyword can be used to override default behavior by explicitly forcing an element to inherit a value from its parent

Choosing font styles

This chapter demonstrates how CSS style rules can suggest a particular font for the display of an element's content and how they can specify the size, weight and angle of its appearance.

Covers

Chapter Five

Suggesting font preference

A CSS style rule can suggest a specific font to be used by the browser for the display of text content of a target element by assigning the font name to its CSS font-family property. The browser will use the specified font if it is available on the user's system – otherwise it will display the text using its default font.

The default font may not be the best choice for the author's purpose so CSS additionally allows the font-family property to suggest a generic font family from those in the table below:

Develop the habit of enclosing all named fonts within quotes.

Font Family	Description	Example
serif	Proportional fonts, where characters have different widths to suit their size, and with serif decorations at the end of the character strokes	Times New Roman
sans-serif	Proportional fonts without serif decorations	Arial
monospace	Non-proportional fonts where characters are of fixed width, similar to type-written text	Courier
cursive	Fonts that attempt to emulate human hand-written text	Comic Sans
fantasy	Decorative fonts with highly graphic appearance	Castellar

The browser will first try to apply the named font but, in the event that is unavailable, will select a font from those available that most closely matches the characteristics of the generic preference. In this way the appearance of the text should at least approximate the author's intention even without specific font-matching.

In a style rule font-family declaration the preferred font name should appear before the generic font family preference. Multiple named fonts can be specified as a comma-separated list – all before the generic font family preference. It is important to enclose font names that contain a space within quote marks or they will not be recognized.

In this example a specific sans-serif font preference is suggested for the entire paragraph element and further specific font preferences from other font families are suggested for each span element. The browser shot shows that each preferred font has been applied here.

On systems where the named fonts are absent the output will appear different to that below but each part of the text will still appear distinct from each other using the local fonts selected by the browser as being appropriate for each font family.

font-family.html

```
<p>The
<span class = "serif">City of New York</span>
was introduced to professional football on the same day
that the city was introduced to the
<span class = "fantasy">New York Giants</span>.
It was a clear sunny
<span class = "mono">October afternoon in 1925</span>
when the Giants took the field to play against the
<span class = "cursive">Frankford Yellow Jackets</span>
</p>
```

font-family.css

```
p            { font-family: "Arial Narrow"   sans-serif }

.serif       { font-family: "Times New Roman"    serif }
.fantasy     { font-family: "Castellar"        fantasy }
.mono        { font-family: "Courier"        monospace }
.cursive     { font-family: "Rage Italic"      cursive }
```

It is considered good practice to specify a generic font family preference in every font-family declaration.

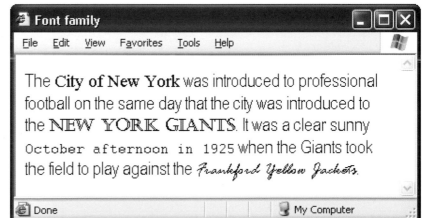

Specifying font size

CSS provides a number of ways to specify a font size to a font-size property in a style rule declaration. The most obvious is as an absolute size, using any of the units listed on page 50 – in, cm, mm, pt or pc. For instance, an absolute size of 12pt like this:

```
#text-1 { font-size: 12pt }
```

Additionally CSS provides the keywords xx-small, x-small, small, medium, large, x-large, and xx-large to specify an absolute size.

keyword	equivalent
xx-large	24pt
x-large	17pt
large	13.5pt
medium	12pt
small	10.5pt
x-small	7.5pt
xx-small	7pt

Here the medium size is determined by the browser's default font size then the rest are computed relative to that size.

Where the default font size is equivalent to 12pt the computed values might look something like those in the table on the left.

Emphasis is made by contrast – specify font sizes using relative terms.

So a style rule declaration might specify a font size one scale higher than the default font size like this:

```
#text-2 { font-size: large }
```

Declarations may also specify a font size one scale higher or lower using the larger and smaller keywords respectively, like this:

```
#text-3 { font-size: larger }
```

Alternatively font size can be specified as a relative size, using any of the unit sizes listed on page 52 – em, ex or px. For instance, double the inherited size (or default size if none is inherited) with a style rule like this:

```
#text-4 { font-size: 2.0em }
```

Similarly font size can be specified as a relative size stated as a percentage. For instance, five times the inherited size like this:

```
#text-5 { font-size: 500% }
```

The example below uses a variety of these methods to display text content in a range of sizes – determined by the absolute and relative values assigned to the elements' font-size properties.

font-size.html

```
<p>This 12pt high text can become
<span class = "lg">larger</span> or
<span class = "sm">smaller</span> <br>
It can get
<span class = "xxl">extremely large</span> or
<span class = "xxs">extremely small</span> <br>
and it may even grow to be
<span class = "huge">huge</span>
</p>
```

font-size.css

```
/* set font size by length */
p      { font-size: 12pt }

/* set font size with keywords */
.lg    { font-size: larger  }
.sm    { font-size: smaller }

.xxl  { font-size: xx-large }
.xxs  { font-size: xx-small }

/* set font size by percentage */
.huge { font-size: 500% }
```

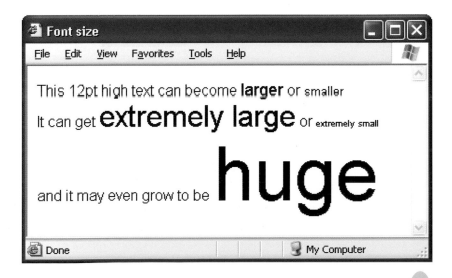

Adjusting font weight

The heaviness or "weight" of a font can easily be adjusted using the CSS font-weight property and the bold and normal keywords.

Assigning a bold value to the font-weight property causes normally weighted text to appear in a heavier font and assigning a normal value causes heavily weighted text to appear in a lighter font. In actuality the browser uses two different fonts to achieve this effect – for normal text it uses a regular weighted font (for instance "Verdana") but it switches to the heavier weighted variant of that font if one is available (such as "Verdana Bold") for bold text.

As an alternative to the bold and normal keywords a font weight can be specified as a numeric value from 100 - 900, by hundreds. A value of 400 is equivalent to normal weight and 700 is equivalent to bold weight.

The font-weight numeric values do not need to specify a unit type because they are effectively keywords.

It is intended that this numeric weighting system should allow for font variants other than the regular and bold ones to be allotted to intermediate values. For instance a font lighter than the regular font (say, "Verdana Light") could equate to the weight value of 300. Similarly a font heavier than the bold font ("Verdana Bold Black") could equate to the numeric weight value of 800.

In practice the numeric system typically uses the regular font for values of 100, 200, 300, 400, 500, and the bold font for values of 600, 700, 800, 900.

CSS provides the keywords bolder and lighter for the purpose of moving up or down the font weight ladder by single steps – but where the browser only recognizes two fonts, for regular and bold text, these have the same effect as the normal and bold keywords.

In the example on the facing page numeric values are used to specify the font weight for each paragraph. The bold and normal keywords are used to switch to the opposite font variant for span elements in each paragraph. Other span elements are styled using the bolder and lighter keywords which require the browser to select an alternative font based on the current font weight.

font-weight.html

```
<p id = "para-1">
This normal weight text can become
<span class = "bold"> bold </span>or
<span class = "more"> bolder </span>
</p>

<p id = "para-2">
This bold weight text can get
<span class = "norm"> light </span>or
<span class = "less"> lighter </span>
</p>

<h2>...here's a heading with
<span class = "less"> lighter </span>text</h2>
```

font-weight.css

```
/* set regular and bold fonts numerically */
#para-1     { font-weight: 400 }
#para-2     { font-weight: 700 }

/* set regular and bold fonts with keywords */
.bold       { font-weight: bold   }
.norm       { font-weight: normal }

/* set heavier and lighter fonts than parent weight */
.more       { font-weight: bolder }
.less       { font-weight: lighter }
```

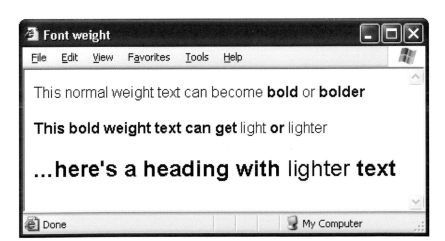

Varying font styles

Slanting text

A CSS font-style property can request the browser to use a slanting variant of the current font by assigning it the italic or oblique keyword values – these are subtly different.

When the italic keyword is used the browser seeks an italicized variant of the current font in its font database. This is an actual font set similar to the current upright font but graphically different to produce slanting versions of each upright character.

When the oblique keyword is used the browser seeks an oblique variant of the current font in its font database. This may be an actual graphical font set, a slanting version of the current upright font, or alternatively it may be a generated version in which the browser has computed a slanting version of the upright font. Either may be mapped to the oblique keyword in the browser's font database and called upon by the CSS font-style property.

In reality using either the italic or oblique keywords typically produces the same italicized text appearance, and in each case upright text can be resumed by assigning the normal keyword to the font-style property.

The small caps font variant

A CSS property called font-variant can be assigned a small-caps value that allows text to be displayed in a popular format using uppercase characters of two different sizes.

Uppercase text in the target element will appear as large capital characters but lowercase text will appear as smaller capitals. The browser may achieve this effect using a smaller capital character from the font set or by generating a computed smaller version.

Once again regular text appearance can be resumed using the normal keyword.

The various font-style and font-variant possibilities are demonstrated in the example opposite which illustrates how a small-caps heading looks and how the italic and oblique text appears identical.

font-style.html

```
<p id = "para-1">
This normal style text can become
<span class = "ital"> italicized </span> or
<span class = "oblq"> oblique </span> </p>

<p id = "para-2">
This italic style text can become
<span class = "reg"> normal </span> </p>

<h2>...And Here's a
<span class = "reg-caps"> Heading </span>
with Small Caps</h2>
```

font-style.css

```
/* set font styles */
#para-1       { font-style: normal      }
#para-2       { font-style: italic      }

.ital         { font-style: italic      }
.oblq         { font-style: oblique     }
.reg          { font-style: normal      }

/* apply small caps variant */
h2            { font-variant: small-caps }
.reg-caps     { font-variant: normal    }
```

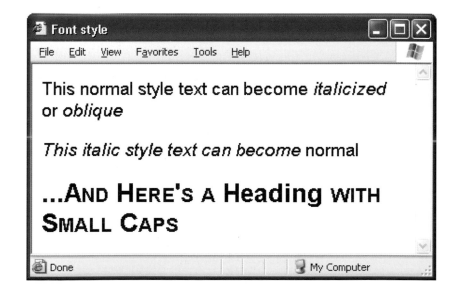

Using the font shorthand

Usefully CSS provides a font property to which various font preferences can be assigned in a combined single rule stating:

font-style | font-variant | font-weight | font-size | font-family

Appropriate values can be assigned to each part of the combined font property, as seen in this rule:

```
p { font: italic small-caps bold medium "Times" serif }
```

The first three values for the font-style, font-variant and font-weight properties may appear in any order. Additionally, they may optionally be omitted. and a normal value will be automatically assumed for those values.

It is important to recognize that values not explicitly specified will still have a normal value applied – the parent value is not inherited, and this can produce some unexpected results. For instance, a font rule targeting a span element within the paragraph styled by the rule above might look like this:

```
span { font: large cursive }
```

The values explicitly specified in this rule will be applied to the font-size and font-family properties and a normal value will be applied to the font-style, font-variant and font-weight properties – so text within the span element is not italic, small-caps, or bold.

One further possibility available with the combined font rule is the option to specify a line-height (the spacing between each line) by adding a forward slash and unit value after the font-weight value. This is useful to establish a common standard line spacing where various font sizes appear. A line-height value of 1.3em is used in the following example that styles a paragraph and a number of child span elements with combined font shorthand style rules.

font-shorthand.css

```
.headr { font: 350% "Pristina" cursive }
.genrl { font: normal small/1.3em "Courier" monospace }
.giant { font: small-caps large "Castellar" fantasy }
.bears { font: large "Arial" sans-serif }
.score { font: bold small "Verdana" sans-serif }
.stadm { font: italic medium "Arial" sans-serif }
.coach { font: medium "Comic Sans MS" cursive }
```

font-shorthand.html

```
<p     class = "genrl">
<span class = "headr"> The Sneakers Game </span>
<br>In 1934 the
<span class = "giant"> New York Giants </span> beat the
<span class = "bears"> Chicago Bears </span>, by
<span class = "score"> 30-13 </span>,
in nine-degree temperatures [
<span class = "stadm"> at the Polo Grounds </span>]
in a game that has become famous as the "Sneakers
Game." With the
<span class = "giant"> Giants </span> trailing
<span class = "score"> 10-3 </span> at the half,
head coach
<span class = "coach"> Steve Owen </span>
provided his squad with basketball shoes to increase
traction on the icy turf. The team responded with four
touchdowns in the second half to turn the game into a
<span class = "giant"> Giants </span> rout.
</p>
```

A font shorthand rule should always contain explicit values for the font-weight and font-family properties.

Summary

- The CSS font-family property can suggest to the browser a specific font to be used to display text in the target element

- Each font-family rule should specify a preferred default family using the keywords serif, sans-serif, monospace, cursive or fantasy

- The CSS font-size property can specify the font size in absolute terms using unit values of in, cm, mm, pt, or pc or using keywords xx-small, x-small, small, medium, large, x-large, or xx-large

- The CSS font-weight property can specify the font weight using the keywords normal, bold, bolder or lighter or using numerical keyword values of 100, 200, 300, 400, 500, 600, 700, 800, or 900

- The CSS font-style property can specify the font angle using the keywords normal, italic, or oblique

- The CSS font-variant property can be assigned the small-caps keyword to display text in two uppercase font sizes

- The CSS font shorthand property provides the ability to specify font-style, font-variant, font-weight, font-size, and font-family values in a single combined rule

- In a font shorthand rule the font-style, font-variant, and font-weight values may appear in any order and may be omitted – in which case a normal value will be automatically assumed

- The font-size component of a font shorthand rule may optionally specify a line-height value for the spacing between lines of text

Controlling text content

This chapter describes the CSS text properties that determine how text content is positioned relative to other line content. It demonstrates, by example, how these can be used to control alignment, indentation, spacing, decoration, and text direction.

Chapter Six

Aligning horizontally

In the English language text content of a paragraph is normally aligned to the left edge of the paragraph and this is the default behavior adopted to display text content in an HTML **p** element.

The text-align property is not equivalent to the HTML <center> element – it only controls the alignment of content within an element, not the alignment of elements within a page. See page 106 for details on how to center elements within a page.

Additionally, CSS provides a **text-align** property that can explicitly specify how lines of text should be aligned within the paragraph boundaries using the keywords **left**, **center**, **right** or **justify**. As expected the **left** value aligns each line to the paragraph's left edge, the **right** value aligns each line to the paragraph's right edge, and the **center** value aligns each line centrally between both edges.

Perhaps more interestingly, the **justify** value aligns each full line to both left and right edges of the paragraph, and also adjusts the spacing between the characters and words to make each line the same length.

This example aligns the text lines of four paragraphs using the **text-align** property. Each paragraph is styled with a colored background to indicate where its edges lie and to demonstrate how the **text-align** style rules align to those edges in each case:

align-horizontal.html

```
<p id = "para-1">
<span class = "label">Left-aligned paragraph:</span>
<br> Enjoy the sunsets, the restaurants, the fishing,
the diving... the lifestyle of the Florida Keys!</p>

<p id = "para-2">
<span class = "label">Right-aligned paragraph:</span>
<br> Enjoy the sunsets, the restaurants, the fishing,
the diving... the lifestyle of the Florida Keys!</p>

<p id = "para-3">
<span class = "label">Center-aligned paragraph:</span>
<br> Enjoy the sunsets, the restaurants, the fishing,
the diving... the lifestyle of the Florida Keys!</p>

<p id = "para-4">
<span class = "label">Justify-aligned paragraph:</span>
<br> Enjoy the sunsets, the restaurants, the fishing,
the diving... the lifestyle of the Florida Keys!</p>
```

align-horizontal.css

```
/* set color and font preferences */
p               { background: yellow;
                  font: medium "Courier" monospace }

span.label      { background: orange;
                  color: white;
                  font-weight: bold            }

/* set paragraph text lines alignment */
p#para-1        { text-align: left            }
p#para-2        { text-align: right           }
p#para-3        { text-align: center          }
p#para-4        { text-align: justify         }
```

Horizontal alignment

File   Edit   View   Favorites   Tools   Help

Left-aligned paragraph:
Enjoy the sunsets, the restaurants, the
fishing, the diving... the lifestyle of the
Florida Keys!

Right-aligned paragraph:
Enjoy the sunsets, the restaurants, the
fishing, the diving... the lifestyle of the
Florida Keys!

Center-aligned paragraph:
Enjoy the sunsets, the restaurants, the
fishing, the diving... the lifestyle of the
Florida Keys!

Justify-aligned paragraph:
Enjoy   the   sunsets,   the   restaurants,   the
fishing,   the   diving...   the   lifestyle   of   the
Florida Keys!

Done   My Computer

Aligning vertically

In displaying a line of text the browser first determines what height the line should be. This may be explicitly specified using the CSS line-height property, otherwise the browser automatically computes the line height to suit the content size – typically this will be 1.2 times the height of the given font. The browser then displays the text within invisible "line boxes", of the required line height, allowing some space both above and below the characters.

The CSS vertical-align property can explicitly specify how content should be vertically aligned to the line box using the keywords baseline, super and sub. The bottom edge of a line box is called the "base line" and assigning the baseline keyword in a style rule aligns the target content with the bottom of the line box.

Usually subscript and superscript is much smaller than the text – create the vertical shift with the sub or super keywords then apply a font rule to reduce the shifted text's size.

The super and sub keywords can be used to create superscript and subscript text by shifting target content up and down respectively. This moves that content outside the line box so the browser increases the boundaries of the outer container in which the line box exists. For instance, lines of text in a paragraph are displayed in individual line boxes that exist within the paragraph container – adding subscript or superscript vertically increases the paragraph boundaries to accommodate the additional height.

Content can also be shifted up or down by assigning positive or negative unit, or percentage, values to the vertical-align property. The top, middle, and bottom keywords can be used to vertically align with the top-most, middle, and bottom-most content.

Two additional keywords, text-top and text-bottom, allow other inline elements such as img image elements to be aligned to the top or bottom edge of the line box.

All the possible vertical-align possibilities are demonstrated in the example opposite that has three paragraph container elements, each holding one line box. The boundaries of each paragraph are visible against the colored background of the document body. Normally these would fit snugly around each line box but they have been automatically increased here by the browser to accommodate content that extends vertically beyond the boundaries of the line boxes.

align-vertical.html

```
<p>Line 1    <span class = "base">baseline</span>
             <span class = "sub">sub</span>
             <span class =" super">super</span> </p>
<p>Line 2    <span class = "plus">+30px</span>
             <span class = "minus">-200%</span>
             <span class = "top">top</span>
             <span class = "mid">middle</span>
             <span class = "btm">bottom</span> </p>
<p>Line 3    <img id = "img-1" src = "txt-top.gif">
             <span class = "base">baseline</span>
             <img id = "img-2" src = "txt-btm.gif"> </p>
```

align-vertical.css

```
.base      { vertical-align: baseline       }
.sub       { vertical-align: sub            }
.super     { vertical-align: super          }
.plus      { vertical-align: 30px           }
.minus     { vertical-align: -200%          }
.top       { vertical-align: top            }
.mid       { vertical-align: middle         }
.btm       { vertical-align: bottom         }
#img-1     { vertical-align: text-top       }
#img-2     { vertical-align: text-bottom    }
```

Indenting and spacing

One of the most common features of printed text is the indentation of the first line of each paragraph to improve readability. This can be easily accomplished for text in HTML paragraphs using the CSS text-indent property to specify an indent size as a unit value, such as 25px.

Alternatively the value can be specified as a percentage where the browser will indent an amount relative to the total line length. For instance, given a paragraph within a div element 500px wide specifying a text-indent value of 10% would indent the start of the first line by 50px (500 x 10% = 50).

It is possible to specify negative values for the text-indent property but this can produce inconsistent results so is best avoided.

The amount of space between each word can be adjusted using the CSS word-spacing property to increase, or decrease, the normal default spacing by a specified unit value, such as 5px. Notice that the rule adjusts the normal spacing so that, in this case, the word spacing becomes (normal space + 5px), not 5px overall.

The word-spacing and letter-spacing properties can both accept negative values – to produce some interesting results.

Similarly, the amount of space between each letter can be adjusted using the CSS letter-spacing property in the same way that the word-spacing property can adjust the spacing between words.

Both word-spacing and letter-spacing properties accept the normal keyword to resume their respective default spacing value. Also, they may both be overridden by a text-align rule (see page 70) that has precedence in determining the appearance of the entire line.

The example on the facing page contains two paragraphs that each begin with an indentation using the CSS text-indent property. The letter-spacing property is used to adjust the spacing between each letter in targeted span elements in both paragraphs. The spacing between words in the final span element of the second paragraph is increased using the word-spacing property.

indent-space.html

```
<p>The Geologic Story at the
<span class = "spread">Grand Canyon</span>
attracts the attention of the world for many reasons,
but perhaps its greatest significance lies in the
geologic record preserved and exposed here.</p>

<p>The rocks at
<span class = "spread">Grand Canyon</span>
are not inherently unique - similar rocks are found
throughout the world. What is unique about the geologic
record at <span class = "spread">Grand Canyon</span>
is the:<span class = "space"><br>variety of
rocks present<br>clarity with which they are
exposed<br>complex geologic story they tell.</span></p>
```

indent-space.css

```
/* set paragraph indent and font */
p        { text-indent: 2em; font: medium monospace    }

/* 50% extra-space lettering */
.spread { letter-spacing: 0.5em; background: yellow }

/* 150% extra-space words */
.space   { word-spacing: 1.5em; background: aqua        }
```

Indenting and spacing text

File Edit View Favorites Tools Help

    The Geologic Story at the G r a n d
C a n y o n attracts the attention of the world
for many reasons, but perhaps its greatest
significance lies in the geologic record
preserved and exposed here.

    The rocks at G r a n d C a n y o n are not
inherently unique — similar rocks are found
throughout the world. What is unique about the
geologic record at G r a n d C a n y o n is the:
variety   of   rocks   present
clarity   with   which   they   are   exposed
complex   geologic   story   they   tell.

Done   My Computer

Decorating text

Style rules can add decorative lines to text content using the CSS text-decoration property with keywords underline, overline, and line-through. These behave, as expected, adding a line below, through, or over, the targeted text respectively.

The blink keyword may also be assigned to the text-decoration property to cause the browser to alternately hide and display the targeted text, "blinking" the text on and off.

Some users may not recognize hyperlinks if their default underline is removed.

More usefully the CSS none keyword can be assigned to the text-decoration property to prevent unwanted decorations appearing – this is particular popular for displaying hyperlinks without their usual default underline.

An additional way to enhance text with CSS is available using its text-transform property to specify the capitalization of the targeted text with the keywords uppercase, lowercase, and capitalize.

The rules in the style sheet below target various elements in the HTML code on the opposite page to enhance textual appearance using both text-decoration and text-transform properties:

enhance-text.css

```
/* set text decoration classes */
.plain { text-decoration: none           }
.under { text-decoration: underline     }
.thru  { text-decoration: line-through }
.rails { text-decoration: overline underline blink   }

/* set text transform classes */
.lower { text-transform: lowercase     }
.upper { text-transform: uppercase     }
.caps  { text-transform: capitalize     }
```

Notice that multiple keywords can be assigned to the text-decoration property as a space-separated list when more than one enhancement is required, as seen here in the rails class.

Similarly, more than one class can be assigned to the HTML class attribute as a space-separated list, such as "under caps".

enhance-text.html

```
<p id = "para-1">You know that it's
<span class = "under caps">important</span>
when <br>it is
<span class = "under">underlined</span>
<br>and that it's been
<span class = "thru caps">cancelled</span>
when <br>it has been
<span class = "thru">struck through</span>
<br>but you also must remember to<br><br>
<span class = "rails upper">read between the lines
</span> <br><br>
for not all of man's intentions
<br>are plain communications.<br>
<span id = "sig" class = "lower">-MIKE MCGRATH</span>
</p> <hr>
<p>
<a href = "http://w3c.org">Regular link</a> |
<a class = "plain" href = "http://w3c.org">
Plain link</a> </p>
```

Use the blink value very sparingly or not at all – it's effect is unliked by most people and despised by many.

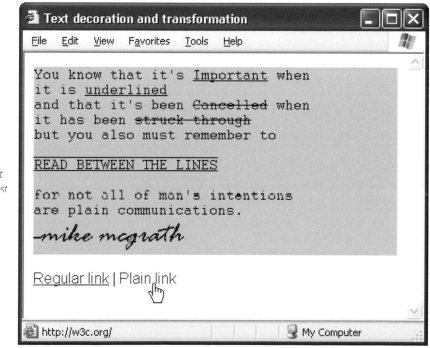

Governing space and direction

The default treatment of whitespace within text content is to collapse multiple spaces into a single space, but this can be controlled with the CSS white-space property. Assigning it the pre keyword preserves all spaces as they appear in the original text, including carriage returns. Conversely the automatic wrapping of text in a block can be prevented by assigning the nowrap keyword. Also the pre-wrap keyword can be assigned to preserve spaces while still allowing text to wrap normally, or the pre-line keyword used to collapse multiple spaces while preserving carriage returns.

The default left-to-right direction of text lines can be changed to right-to-left by assigning the rtl keyword to the CSS direction property, and the normal direction resumed with the ltr keyword.

Interestingly, when the line direction is changed with rtl the words appear from right-to-left but the order of the English characters are preserved so that each word still reads correctly left-to-right.

You can discover more about Unicode character code online at www.unicode.org.

This intelligent feature also allows text to be presented in different directions on a single line, for example to incorporate words in languages that are read right-to-left such as Hebrew and Arabic. The browser examines the Unicode value of each character using a complex BiDirectional algorithm to determine which direction each word should be displayed – those characters from right-to-left languages are automatically displayed in that direction, even if written logically, from left-to-right, in the HTML source code. CSS allows the automatic BiDirectional algorithm to be turned off by assigning the bidi-override keyword to a unicode-bidi property.

The following example begins by displaying a paragraph containing preserved whitespace and Hebrew text that is automatically reversed from its logical HTML order to be displayed right-to-left. Further style rules demonstrate the effect of changing the line direction and of overriding the Unicode BiDirectional algorithm

space-direction.css

```
/* preserve whitespace in paragraphs   */
p              { white-space: pre          }

/* direction and bidi override classes */
.ltr           { direction: ltr            }
.rtl           { direction: rtl            }
.bidi-off      { unicode-bidi: bidi-override   }
```

space-direction.html

```
<p>Hebrew "Congratulations" with mazel tov:
 &#1502;&#1494;&#1500;  [ mazel]
   + &#1496;&#1493;&#1489;  [ tov]
     = &#1502;&#1494;&#1500;  &#1496;&#1493;&#1489;;
</p>

<dl>
<dt>LTR Default Direction(lines begin at the LEFT)</dt>
<dd class = "ltr">&#1502;&#1494;&#1500; [ mazel]
&#1496;&#1493;&#1489; [ tov] </dd>

<dt>RTL Custom Direction(lines begin at the RIGHT)</dt>
<dd class = "rtl">&#1502;&#1494;&#1500; [ mazel]
&#1496;&#1493;&#1489; [ tov] </dd>

<dt>LTR ExplicitDirection+BiDirectional Override:</dt>
<dd class = "bidi-off ltr">No longer reads as mazel tov
: &#1502;&#1494;&#1500;  &#1496;&#1493;&#1489;;</dd>
</dl>
```

The numerical values in this code are the character entity values for the Hebrew characters – more on character entities online at www.w3.org.

Generally the default treatment of right-to-left language characters achieves the desired effect. Overriding the Unicode BiDirectional algorithm is seldom needed in the real world.

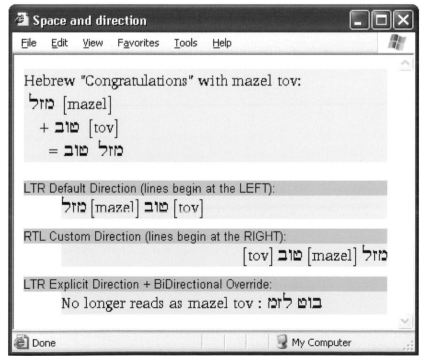

Summary

- Text can be horizontally aligned to its container edges using the CSS text-align property and keywords left, center, right, or justify

- The height of text lines can be explicitly specified by assigning a unit size to the line-height property

- A web browser displays text within invisible line boxes which it creates to fit the size of text on that line

- Text can be vertically aligned to a line box using the CSS vertical-align property and the keywords baseline, super, sub, top, middle, bottom, text-top, or text-bottom

- The first line of a paragraph can be indented by assigning a unit value to the text-indent property

- The amount of space between letters can be adjusted using the letter-spacing property and the amount of space between words can be adjusted using the word-spacing property

- Text can be enhanced using the CSS text-decoration property and the keywords underline, overline, line-through, or none

- Capitalization can be specified to the text-transform property using the keywords uppercase, lowercase, or capitalize

- Spaces and carriage returns in text can be preserved using the white-space property and the keywords pre, pre-line, pre-wrap, or nowrap

- The direction in which text lines are displayed can be specified using the direction property and the ltr or rtl keywords

- The unicode-bidi property and bidi-override keyword can be used to turn off the browser's BiDirectional algorithm — allowing explicit control of text direction by the CSS direction property

Understanding content boxes

This chapter explains the content box model used by browsers to display content on a web page. Examples demonstrate how to control both block-level boxes and inline-boxes using style rules.

Covers

Chapter Seven

The block content box

CSS considers each HTML element to generate an invisible rectangular box to contain its content – a "content box".

Block-level elements are those HTML elements, such as paragraph, heading, and div elements, that automatically generate a new line both before and after their boxes. These "block content boxes" will normally appear stacked vertically, one below another.

Each block content box comprises a core content area surrounded by optional areas of padding, border, and margin, as shown here:

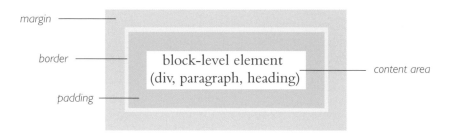

When the padding, border, and margin areas each have zero width the content box will be the same size as the content area – determined by the space needed by the dimensions of its content.

Any padding, border, and margin areas that have a non-zero width are added outside the content area – so the content area size remains the same but the content box size increases.

The CSS padding property can be assigned a unit value to create an extended area immediately surrounding the content area. The padding area will inherit the background color of that content area.

Full details on styling content boxes are given in the next chapter.

A CSS border property can specify a border-style, width, and color, to create an extended area surrounding the content area – and its padding area if applicable.

A margin property can be assigned a unit value to create an extended transparent area surrounding the content area – and its padding area and border area where applicable.

The example opposite first creates a basic paragraph content box then adds each of the optional content box areas in successive paragraph content boxes.

block-boxes.html

```
<p >Content Box</p>

<p class = "pad">Content Box (padded)</p>

<p class = "pad bdr">Content Box (padded + border)</p>

<p class = "pad bdr mgn">
Content Box (padded + border + margin)</p>
```

block-boxes.css

```
/* default paragraph styles */
p      { width: 250px; background: lime }

/* add a padding area */
p.pad { padding: 10px }

/* add a border area */
p.bdr { border: solid fuchsia 10px }

/* add a margin area */
p.mgn { margin: 40px }
```

Padding, border, and margin areas are added outside the content area without changing its original size.

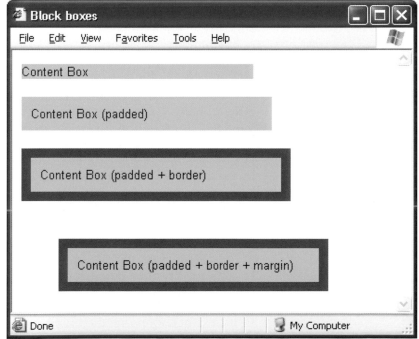

The inline content box

As stated when introducing block content boxes, CSS considers each HTML element to generate an invisible rectangular "content box" – and this consideration includes non block-level elements.

Inline-level elements are those HTML elements contained within block-level elements, such as span, a, and img elements, that do not automatically generate a new line before and after their boxes. The "inline content boxes" will normally appear in-line horizontally, one after another.

Inline content boxes are created for each of these content types:

- Non-replaced elements, such as span and a elements, whose tag content appears literally in the document

- Replaced elements, such as img and form input elements, which are placeholders for non-textual items that are displayed in the document

- Anonymous text, such as text within a p paragraph element, which appears literally in the document

The width of the inline content box will extend horizontally to accommodate the width of its content and its height will be determined by the height of its content.

Don't confuse line boxes – which determine text alignment to a baseline (see page 72) with inline content boxes – which determine the layout of content inside a block.

For anonymous text and non-replaced elements the height of the inline content box is governed by the tallest font-size in that box – the line box height of the tallest text.

For replaced elements the inline content box height is governed by the height of the non-textual replacement – the height of the image in the case of an inline img element.

It is important to recognize that the height of an inline content box that contains a replaced element will include any areas of padding, border, or margin, in addition to its core content area. In contrast, an inline box that contains anonymous text or non-replaced element will not include any extended areas.

In the example opposite the inline content box height accommodates the extended areas of the (replaced) second img element but not those of the (non-replaced) second a element.

inline-boxes.html

```
<p>
Here is some anonymous text inside the p tag with a
<span class = "reg">non-replaced span element</span>
and a <a class = "reg" href = "#">non-replaced anchor
element</a>.There is also a replaced
<img class = "reg" src = "box.gif"> image element. See
how the line height automatically accommodates its
tallest item. This includes padding, border, and margin
areas of replaced elements, like this image element
<img class= "ext" src= "box.gif">  - but not those of
non-replaced elements, like this
<a class = "ext" href="#">anchor element</a>
</p>
```

inline-boxes.css

```css
span  { font-size: x-large }

/* regular area - without padding, border & margin */
.reg  { background: lime }

/* extended area - with padding, border & margin */
.ext  { padding: 4px; border: 1px solid red;
        margin: 4px; background: yellow }
```

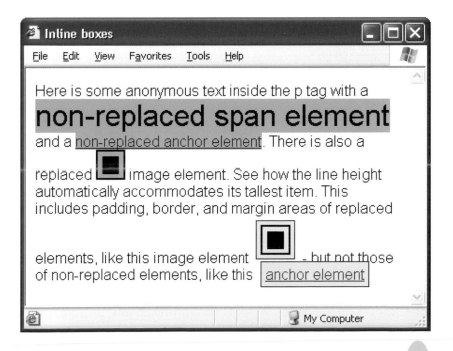

Changing display formats

The previous two examples illustrate how the display format of a document relies upon the creation of block content boxes to determine its general layout and the creation of inline content boxes within those block boxes to determine its precise layout

This places great emphasis on whether an element is considered as block-level or inline-level to decide the appropriate display format.

Usually the default display type will be the appropriate format. For instance, it's generally desirable to display list items on individual lines. But explicitly assigning the CSS block or inline keywords to an element's display property, changing it from its default value, can change the display format of a document.

This means that content can be displayed in alternative ways without changing the HTML tags. To illustrate how this can be useful the following example displays a list of items vertically, using the default display style, and horizontally, using a custom display style. Similarly, it shows a sequence of links in the default horizontal inline format then in a custom vertical block format:

change-display.css

```
<dl>
<dt>Block (default)
<dd>Item 1<dd>Item 2<dd>Item 3
</dl>

<dl class = "line-up">
<dt>Inline (custom)
<dd>Item 1<dd>Item 2<dd>Item 3
</dl>

<p>Inline (default)
<a href = "page-1.html">Page 1</a>
<a href = "page-2.html">Page 2</a>
<a href = "page-3.html">Page 3</a>
</p>

<p class = "block-up">Block (custom)
<a href = "page-1.html">Page 1</a>
<a href = "page-2.html">Page 2</a>
<a href = "page-3.html">Page 3</a>
</p>
```

change-display.css

```
/* show borders of containers */
p,dl  { border: 1px solid silver }

/* color the components to be changed */
a      { background: lime  }
dd     { background: aqua  }

/* change from the default display types */
.block-up a   { display: block  }
.line-up dd   { display: inline }
```

Unless a width is specified a block content box will extend to the boundary of its containing element – an inline content-box is just big enough for its content.

Change display formats

File   Edit   View   Favorites   Tools   Help

Block (default)
   Item 1
   Item 2
   Item 3

Inline (custom)
   Item 1   Item 2   Item 3

Inline (default) Page 1 Page 2 Page 3

Block (custom)
Page 1
Page 2
Page 3

My Computer

It should be noted that assigning a non-default display value to an element only changes the way it gets displayed – it does not actually change its default display type. Inline elements are always descendants of block-level elements in the document tree. Block-level elements can never be descendants of inline elements, even when the display property of the block-level element has been assigned an inline value.

Creating special blocks

In addition to the block value and inline value the CSS display property offers two further possible values which can be used to create special content boxes:

Run-in style

The run-in value can be assigned to the display property in a style rule that targets a block-level element which is followed by another block-level element. When the rule is applied it has the effect of changing the block content box of the first element into an inline content box – apparently displaying the combined content inline. For instance, targeting a heading element which is followed by a paragraph element will force the heading content to appear inline with the start of the paragraph content.

The run-in style can only be used on a block content box where the next box is also a block content box.

This effect is demonstrated in the example below which applies a run-in style to a h3 heading element, causing its content to appear inline with that of the subsequent p paragraph element:

run-in-boxes.html

```
<h3 class>Heading Block (Default)</h3>
<p>Paragraph Block with simple plain text content</p>

<h3 class = "runin-blox">Heading Block (Run-in)</h3>
<p>Paragraph Block with simple plain text content</p>
```

run-in-boxes.css

```
p      { background: yellow      }
h3     { background: lime        }

.runin-blox { display: run-in    }
```

This example is illustrated with the Firefox web browser – the appearance may vary with Internet Explorer.

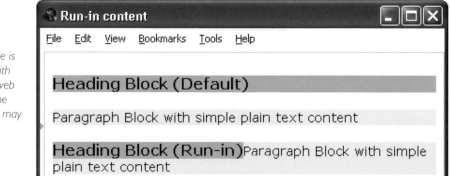

Inline-block style

The inline-block value can be assigned to the display property in a style rule that targets an inline-level element to change the internal behavior of inline content boxes to that of block content boxes.

The run-in and inline-block styles are not universally supported so it may be best to avoid using them – they are included here for completeness.

This means that while inline-block content boxes still appear inline, like regular inline content boxes, their content can be formatted as though it was block-level. For instance, style rules can specify width and height values for an inline-block content box.

In the example below a style rule targets the a anchor elements to create inline-block boxes for their content, specifying their width and centering the text content within each inline-block box.

inline-block-boxes.html

```
<p>Inline Content Boxes (default)
<a href = "page-1.html">Page 1</a>
<a href = "page-2.html">Page 2</a>
<a href = "page-3.html">Page 3</a> </p>

<p class = "inline-blox">
Inline Block Content Boxes (custom)
<a href = "page-1.html">Page 1</a>
<a href = "page-2.html">Page 2</a>
<a href = "page-3.html">Page 3</a> </p>
```

inline-block-boxes.css

```
p       { background: orange }
a       { background: aqua   }

.inline-blox a { display: inline-block;
                 width: 32%; text-align: center }
```

Summary

- CSS considers each HTML element to generate an invisible rectangular content box

- Block-level elements generate block content boxes which normally appear stacked vertically, one below another

- Each block content box comprises a core content area plus optional padding, border, and margin areas, which are added outside the core content area of a block content box

- Inline-level elements generate inline content boxes which normally appear inline horizontally, one after another

- Each inline content box may contain a replaced element, non-replaced element, or anonymous text content

- Where an inline content box contains a non-replaced element or anonymous text its height is determined by the tallest font-size

- Where an inline content box contains a replaced element its height is determined by the tallest non-textual replacement – including any padding, border, and margin areas

- An inline content box is just wide enough to fit its content but an unrestrained block content box will extend to the boundary of its containing outer element

- Default display formats can be changed by explicitly assigning block or inline values to an element's display property

- The run-in value can be assigned to the display property to display one block content box inline with a second block content box

- Assigning an inline-block value to an inline-level element's display property creates an inline-block content box – displayed inline but whose contents can be formatted like a block content box

Styling content boxes

This chapter demonstrates how to implement style rules to add padding, borders, and margins, around the core content box area. Examples illustrate how a single rule can specify the appearance around all four sides and how each side can be styled individually.

Covers

Chapter Eight

Specifying border styles

Using the box model introduced in the last chapter (see below) style rules can specify the appearance of each optional extended area around an element's core content area.

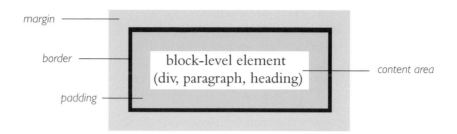

The border area surrounds the core content area and padding area so that the overall element background will extend to the outer edges of the border area.

In CSS each border comprises a border-width, border-color, and border-style. The default border-width is medium (a computed value) and its border-color is inherited from the element's color value, but the initial border-style is none – so the border is not visible until the border-style property is explicitly assigned a value. Possible values are solid, double, dotted, dashed, groove, ridge, inset, outset, none, and hidden.

The border-width and border-color properties may also be assigned explicit values to change from their default value.

Specifying borders in this way applies the same appearance to all four sides of the border but individual properties of each side can be targeted separately. For instance, each side's border-style can be specified independently as border-top-style, border-bottom-style, border-left-style and border-right-style properties.

Similarly, each side's border-width can be specified independently as border-top-width, border-bottom-width, etc. and each side's border-color as border-top-color, border-bottom-color, etc..

The border around the first paragraph in the example opposite is displayed simply by specifying a border-style value – it uses the default border-width and inherited border-color values. The other paragraph borders display their explicitly specified values.

The extent of an element's background can be clearly seen through the spaces in an intermittent border-style, such as a dashed line.

border-styles.html

border-styles.css

```html
<p id = "p-1">solid - inherit - medium</p>
<p id = "p-2">outset - yellow - 10px</p>
<p id = "p-3">double - blue - 20px</p>
<p id = "p-4">top: dotted - orange - 10px
<br>bottom: dashed - green - 20px</p>
```

```css
#p-1  { color: red; border-style: solid                    }

#p-2  { border-style: outset;
        border-color: yellow; border-width: 10px      }

#p-3  { border-style: double;
        border-color: blue; border-width: 20px         }

#p-4  { border-top-style: dotted;
        border-top-color: orange;
        border-top-width: 10px;
        border-bottom-style: dashed;
        border-bottom-color: green;
        border-bottom-width: 20px; background: aqua  }
```

The outset border-style can be used to create the appearance of a raised button – and the inset border-style can be used to create the appearance of a depressed button.

Border styles — File Edit View Favorites Tools Help

solid - inherit - medium

outset - yellow - 10px

double - blue - 20px

top: dotted - orange - 10px
bottom: dashed - green - 20px

Done   My Computer

Using the border shorthand

The variety of border properties available in CSS allows very precise control over the color, style, and width, of the individual border appearance on each side of the core content area – but specifying style rules for each separate aspect can become tedious. Fortunately CSS also provides "shorthand" properties where multiple aspects can be specified in a single rule.

Multiple property shorthand

The border shorthand property can be assigned border-width, border-style, and border-color, values as a space-separated list to specify the border appearance on all four sides. So a single border shorthand rule effectively specifies three property values at once.

Of all the many border options the border shorthand is probably the one most used by web page authors.

Similarly, the border-top, border-right, border-bottom, and border-left shorthand properties can be assigned border-width, border-style, and border-color, values as a space-separated list to specify the individual border on each side of the content area. These each effectively specify three property values in a single rule for each border side.

Multiple value shorthand

Another possible shorthand technique provided by CSS is the ability to assign multiple values to the border-width, border-style, and border-color properties as a space-separated list. These can each specify one, two, three or, four values in a single rule.

The number of assigned values determine how they are applied:

- When one value is specified – it is applied to the border on all four sides of the element

- When two values are specified – the first is applied to the top and bottom borders, the second to the left and right borders

- When three values are specified – the first is applied to the top border, the second is applied to both left and right borders, and the third is applied to the bottom border

- When four values are specified – they are applied clockwise to the top, right, bottom, then left borders

The example opposite demonstrates both multiple property border shorthand and multiple value border shorthand:

```html
<p id = "p-1">ridge fuchsia 10px</p>
<p id = "p-2">top - right- bottom - left</p>
<p id = "p-3">styles: dashed solid<br>widths: 20px 10px
<br>colors:red - green - blue - yellow</p>
```

border-shorthands.html

```css
/* multiple property shorthand... */
#p-1 {          border: 10px ridge fuchsia            }

/* individual multiple property shorthands... */
#p-2 {          border-top:     20px groove aqua;
                border-right:   30px solid orange;
                border-bottom:  40px dotted teal;
                border-left:    50px double lime; }

/* multiple value shorthands... } */
#p-3 {          border-style: dashed solid ;
                border-width: 20px 10px;
                border-color: red green blue yellow        }
```

border-shorthands.css

Notice how the browser miters the borders diagonally where they meet – this offers some creative possibilities.

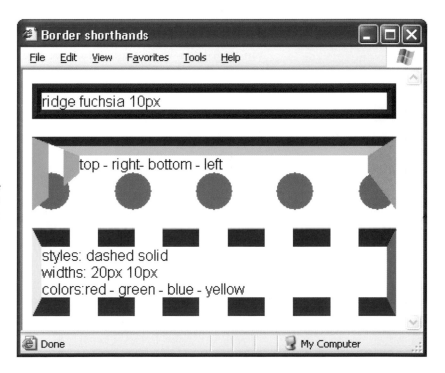

Specifying padding styles

Using the box model, style rules can specify the size of an optional extended padding area around an element's core content area.

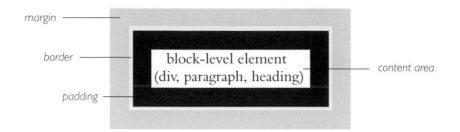

The padding area surrounds the core content area and will extend to the outer edges of the border area, if a border area is specified, right up to the beginning of the margin area. The element's background fills the core content area and the padding area.

The CSS padding property can specify the size as a unit value or as a percentage value. When a percentage value is specified the padding area size is calculated using the width and height values of the outer containing element – and the padding area size will be adjusted if the outer element dimensions get adjusted.

Setting padding as a percentage may produce undesirable results when the user resizes the browser window – use px units to avoid this.

For instance, a padding value of 10% applied to a paragraph contained within a div element of 100px square would create a padding area 10px wide on all four sides of the core content area. Increasing the div to become 200px square automatically increases the padding area to 20px wide on all four sides of the content area.

Typically a padding area is specified when adding a border to an element to increase the distance between the content area and the border – so the content doesn't appear right alongside the border.

This effect is demonstrated in the example opposite which first adds padding to a paragraph to move its content away from the paragraph border area, and then adds padding to a div element to move its content away from the div border area:

padding-styles.html

```
<div id = "d-1">div without padding
<p>Content area without padding</p>
<p class = "pad-pc">Content area with 5% padding</p>
</div>

<div id = "d-2" class = "pad-px">div with 10 px padding
<p>Content area without padding</p>
<p class = "pad-px">Content area with 10px padding</p>
</div>
```

padding-styles.css

```
#d-1  { background: yellow;  border: 3px dashed blue  }
#d-2  { background: lime;    border: 3px dashed blue  }
p     { background: white;   border: 3px dashed red   }

.pad-px { padding: 10px   }
.pad-pc { padding: 5%     }
```

Notice how the background fills the core content area and the padding area – extending up to the outer edge of the border area.

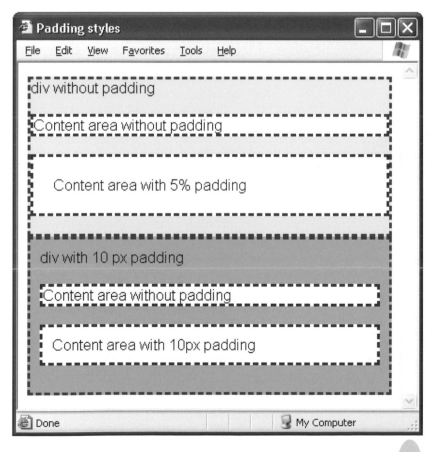

Using the padding shorthand

As with borders, CSS provides properties to set the padding area individually on each side of a content area with padding-top, padding-right, padding-bottom, and padding-left. Each of these can be assigned unit values, or percentage values, to specify the width of an individual padding area around a content box – in much the same that the padding property (described on the previous page) specifies the width of all four padding areas.

Multiple value shorthand

Additionally, the padding property provides a shorthand technique in which it can be assigned multiple values to determine how the padding areas should appear.

The number of assigned values determine how they are applied:

- When one value is specified – padding is applied to all four sides of the element

- When two values are specified – the first is applied to the top and bottom padding areas, the second to the left and right padding areas

- When three values are specified – the first is applied to the top padding area, the second is applied to both left and right padding areas, and the third is applied to the bottom padding area

- When four values are specified – they are applied clockwise to the top, right, bottom, then left padding areas

Of all the many padding options the padding shorthand is probably the one most used by web page authors.

The example opposite demonstrates the application of padding horizontally, to the left and right sides of a content area, and vertically, to the top and bottom sides of a content area.

In the case of the inline content box notice that the padding areas do not increase the line height, but overflow instead. This is true for all non-replaced inline content but replaced elements, such as an inline img image element, will increase the line height to accommodate any extended top or bottom padding areas.

The padding shorthand values applied to the last p element emulate those applied individually in the previous p element.

padding-shorthand.html

```
<p>Content area with horizontally
<span class = "pad-h">padded</span> content</p>

<p>Content area with vertically
<span class = "pad-v">padded</span> content</p>

<p class = "pad-h pad-v">
Content area horizontally and vertically padded</p>

<p class = "pad-4">
Content area padded top, right, bottom, left</p>
```

padding-shorthand.css

```
p      { background: aqua; border: 3px dashed blue }
span   { background: yellow; border: 3px dashed red }

/* pad left and right - individually */
.pad-h       { padding-left: 40px; padding-right: 20px }

/* pad top and bottom - individually */
.pad-v       { padding-top: 10px; padding-bottom: 30px }

/* pad top, right, bottom, left - using shorthand */
.pad-4       { padding: 10px 20px 30px 40px }
```

Horizontal padding areas do not extend beyond the end of a line – they are wrapped to the next line.

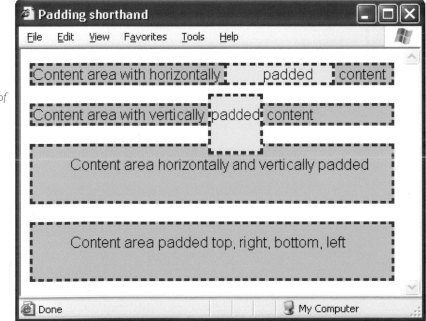

Specifying margin styles

Using the box model, style rules can specify the size of an optional extended margin area around an element.

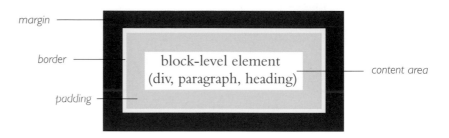

margin

border

padding

block-level element
(div, paragraph, heading)

content area

The margin area is the extreme outer area encompassing the element's core content area, any padding area, and any border area. The margin is always transparent and is used to determine the distance away from surrounding elements.

In CSS the margin property has a zero default value so it's reasonable to expect elements to appear adjacent to each other by default. In reality the browser applies its own intrinsic default margin values to allow space between elements. For instance, heading elements automatically allow a margin area before a following paragraph.

The CSS margin property can specify the size as a unit value, or as a percentage value, or with the keyword auto to have the browser compute the size.

Typically a style rule might seek to control the default margin area created by the browser by assigning the margin property a unit value, or to remove the margin area by assigning it a zero value.

As margins are transparent it is necessary to consider the space between the elements in the following example in order to recognize the margin areas. The example begins by showing the default margins between a heading element and two subsequent paragraph elements - in this case the browser allows margin space to the top or bottom of the elements, not left or right.

Similar elements are then repeated with a style rule fixing the margin size at 5 pixels all round. Finally they are repeated once more with a style rule removing the margin areas entirely:

HOT TIP

The ability to automatically compute the margin size with the auto keyword is essential for centering content – see page 106 for more details.

margin-styles.html

```html
<h2>Heading (default margin)</h2>
<p>Paragraph (default margin)</p>
<p>Paragraph (default margin)</p>

<h2 class = "set-margin">Heading (5px margin)</h2>
<p  class = "set-margin">Paragraph (5px margin)</p>
<p  class = "set-margin">Paragraph (5px margin)</p>

<h2 class = "no-margin">Heading (no margin)</h2>
<p  class = "no-margin">Paragraph (no margin)</p>
<p  class = "no-margin">Paragraph (no margin)</p>
```

margin-styles.css

```css
/* show element boundaries */
h2    { background: aqua   }
p     { background: lime   }

/* classes to control margin size...*/
.set-margin { margin: 5px }

.no-margin  { margin: 0 }
```

Notice how the margin value of 5px below the second heading is <u>combined</u> with the margin value of 5px above the subsequent paragraph, so the total margin size is 5 pixels – the heading margin is <u>not added</u> to the paragraph margin to make a total margin size of 10 pixels.

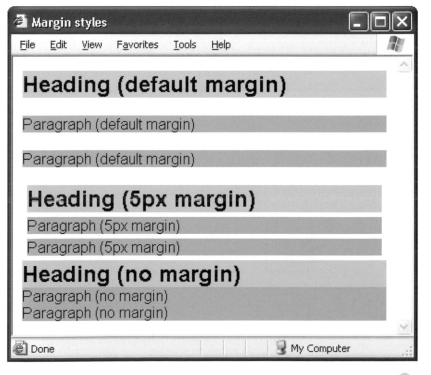

Using the margin shorthand

As with borders and padding, CSS provides properties to set the margin area individually on each side of a content area with margin-top, margin-right, margin-bottom, and margin-left. Each of these can be assigned unit values, or percentage values, to specify the width of an individual margin area around a content box – in much the same that the margin property (described on the previous page) specifies the width of all four margin areas.

Multiple value shorthand
Additionally, the margin property provides a shorthand technique in which it can be assigned multiple values to determine how the margin areas should appear:

- When one value is specified – a margin area is applied to all four sides of the element

Of all the many margin options the margin shorthand is probably the one most used by web page authors.

- When two values are specified – the first is applied to the top and bottom margins, the second to the left and right margins

- When three values are specified – the first is applied to the top margin, the second is applied to both left and right margins, and the third is applied to the bottom margin area

- When four values are specified – they are applied clockwise to the top, right, bottom, then left margin areas

The example below applies top margins to space each div element 10 pixels apart vertically. By default the browser applies top and bottom margins to the heading element and a style rule adds a left margin to the heading in the second div. The margins of the headings in the last two divs are set alike – by individual rules in the third div, and by a shorthand rule in the final div element:

margin-shorthand.html

```
<div>
<h2 class = "def">Heading (default margin)</h2>
</div> <div>
<h2 class = "set-left">Heading (left margin)</h2>
</div> <div>
<h2 class = "set-each">Heading (all margins)</h2>
</div> <div>
<h2 class = "set-all">Heading (margin shorthand)</h2>
</div>
```

margin-shorthand.css

```
/* set top div margins & show container boundaries */
div    { margin-top: 10px; border: 1px solid gray }

.def  { background: lime }

/* set left margin only */
.set-left    { margin-left: 50px; background: yellow }

/* set each margin using individual properties */
.set-each
{
        margin-top: 0px;
        margin-right: 20px;
        margin-bottom: 10px;
        margin-left: 30px;
        background: aqua
}

/* set all margins using margin shorthand */
.set-all {   margin: 0px 20px 10px 30px;
             background: orange }
```

Don't confuse the thin border in this example with the heading element's border property – it is actually the div elements' border property, used here to indicate the heading elements' margin confines.

Summary

- CSS content boxes have optional padding, border, and margin areas that surround the core content area

- The border surrounds the core content and padding areas, and comprises border-width, border-color, and border-style properties

- Automatic values are set for border-width (medium) and border-color (element color) but border-style must explicitly assign solid, double, dotted, dashed ridge, groove, inset, outset, none, or hidden

- Individual borders can be created using side-specific properties such as border-top-style, border-top-width, border-top-color, etc.

- The padding area surrounds the core content area and has a default width of zero

- A padding property can specify the padding area width as a unit value or as a percentage of the containing element's size

- Individual padding can be created using side-specific properties of padding-top, padding-right, padding-bottom, and padding-left

- The margin area surrounds the core content area, padding area, and border area, and has initial values assigned by the browser

- A margin property can specify the margin area width as a unit value, or as a percentage, or with the auto keyword

- Individual margins can be created using side-specific properties of margin-top, margin-right, margin-bottom, and margin-left

- Using border shorthand border-width, border-style and border-color values can be specified as a space-separated list in one rule

- Multiple value shorthand allows padding, border, and margin properties to specify a space-separated list of values in a single rule to apply clockwise to the top, right, bottom, and left sides

Positioning content boxes

This chapter demonstrates how to control the absolute and relative position of block-level content boxes. Style rules are used for automatic horizontal centering and to specify xyz axis coordinates. Examples also illustrate how to control content flow.

Covers

Chapter Nine

Centering content boxes

One of the basic requirements in displaying document components is the ability to horizontally center blocks of content – in the same way provided by the old HTML <center> tag.

In CSS the ability to horizontally center block-level elements is provided by the margin property and the auto keyword.

Assigning an auto value to either margin-top or margin-bottom properties of a block-level element will remove any top or bottom margin – just like assigning them a zero value.

When the auto keyword is assigned to an element's margin property the browser first calculates the distance to the left and right of that element, up to the boundaries of its containing element, then divides the total in half to compute the value of each side margin. For instance, applying an auto margin to a div element of 80px width, that is contained within a second div element of 200px width, the browser divides the total difference of 120px in half to apply 60px margins to each side of the element – so the smaller div element block content box is centered within its larger parent element's block content box.

Notice that the auto margin does not center vertically but merely sets the top and bottom margins to zero, so there are no margin areas above or below the element block.

The auto margin technique is used to horizontally center block-level content boxes and should not be confused with the text-align property that is used to center content within inline-level content boxes.

Both are used in the example on the facing page to demonstrate the difference between their functionality. The first outer div element contains two smaller inner div elements. A style rule targets the second inner div, setting its margin property to auto – centering that div horizontally within the outer div block.

When this browser window gets resized the entire second outer div, gets automatically repositioned to be horizontally centered again.

The second outer div element content box is itself targeted by a style rule that sets its margin property to auto, thereby centering it in the browser window by computing equal side margins up to the containing body element of the document. A style rule targets the second and third inner div element content boxes, centering them horizontally as before, and the inline content box of the third inner div is also targeted by a style rule that assigns a center value to its text-align property to center the inline text content.

center-boxes.html

```html
<div class = "outer-div">Default position
  <div class = "inner-div">Default position</div>
  <div class = "inner-div block-center">
    Centered block content box</div>
</div>

<div class = "outer-div block-center">
  Centered block content box
  <div class = "inner-div">Default position</div>
  <div class = "inner-div block-center">
    Centered block content box</div>
  <div class = "inner-div block-center inline-center">
  Centered block content box + centered inline content
  </div>
</div>
```

center-boxes.css

```css
.outer-div   { width: 270px; border: 1px solid black;
                background: orange; margin-bottom:10px  }
.inner-div   { width: 230px; border: 1px solid black;
                background: yellow                      }

/* center block-level boxes & overwrite background */
.block-center  { margin: auto; background: aqua         }
/* center inline-level boxes & overwrite background */
.inline-center { text-align: center; background: lime }
```

The first outer div element content box has a bottom margin of 10px – just to separate it from the second div element content box for display purposes.

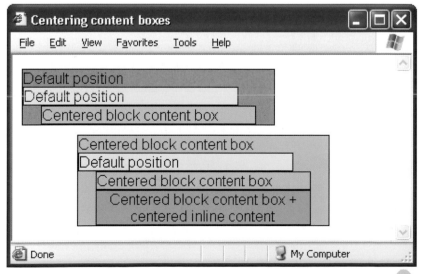

Positioning boxes absolutely

When laying out the element content boxes of a document the CSS position property has a default value of static – representing the normal flow positioning scheme. Assigning a different value to an element's position property can remove that element's content box from the normal flow so it can be positioned independently.

Alternatives to the default static value can be specified using the absolute, relative and fixed keywords to specify an alternative positioning scheme to that of the normal flow layout.

The absolute, relative, and fixed positioning schemes each use one or more of the CSS "offset" properties top, right, bottom, and left, to define their position.

When the position property is specified as absolute the positioning scheme places the element at the specified offset distances from the boundaries of its containing element. For instance, a div element with top and left offset values of 100px will be positioned 100px below and to the right of its container boundaries.

This example demonstrates how the absolute positioning scheme places four outer div elements at the specified offset distances from the boundaries of their containing body element, and four inner div elements at the specified offset distances from the boundaries of their respective containing div element:

absolute-positions.html

```
<div class = "top-left large">top:0 left:0
<div class = "bottom-right small">bottom:0 right:0
</div></div>

<div class = "top-right large">top:0 right:0
<div class = "bottom-left small">bottom:0 left:0
</div></div>

<div class = "bottom-left large">
<br><br><br><br>bottom:0 left:0
<div class = "top-right small">top:0 right:0
</div></div>

<div class = "bottom-right large">
<br><br><br><br>bottom:0 right:0
<div class = "top-left small">top:0 left:0</div></div>
```

absolute-positions.css

```
/* set element sizes & borders */

.large        {        width: 200px; height: 90px;
                       border: 1px solid black        }

.small        {        width: 80px; height: 50px;
                       border: 1px solid black        }

/* specify element positions & backgrounds */

.top-left     {        position: absolute;
                       top:0px; left: 0px;
                       background: lime               }

.top-right    {        position: absolute;
                       top:0px; right: 0px;
                       background: aqua               }

.bottom-left  {        position: absolute;
                       bottom: 0px; left: 0px;
                       background: yellow             }

.bottom-right {        position: absolute;
                       bottom: 0px; right: 0px;
                       background: orange             }
```

 Maximizing this window retains the outer div positions, at each corner of the browser window, and the inner divs remain positioned inside them as seen here.

Absolute positioning

File Edit View Favorites Tools Help

top:0 left:0   top:0 right:0

                bottom:0   bottom:0
                right:0   left:0

                top:0   top:0 left:0
                right:0

bottom:0 left:0   bottom:0 right:0

Done   My Computer

Stacking content boxes

Changing from the static default positioning scheme, by assigning the absolute value to the CSS position property, elements can be positioned to overlap – stacking one above the other in the same order they are listed in the HTML code.

Stack order can be explicitly specified however, by assigning an integer value to the z-index property of each element. The element with the highest value appears uppermost, then beneath that appears the element with the next highest value, and so on.

So the absolute positioning scheme allows element position to be precisely controlled in three dimensions using XYZ coordinates – along the X axis with the left and right offset properties, along the Y axis using the top and bottom offset properties, and along the Z axis using the z-index stack order property:

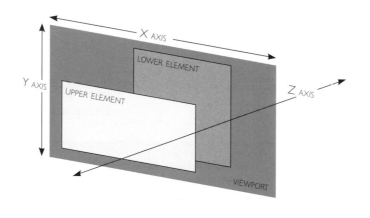

The "viewport" is simply another name for the browser window.

The example opposite assigns a z-index value to several overlapping div elements to determine their stack order. Beneath the uppermost element each lower element is offset by 3px to become lower and to the right of the element above. The element background colors are a progressively lighter shade of gray to create a drop shadow effect beneath the uppermost element.

absolute-stack.html

```html
<div id = "pale-gray"></div>

<div id = "lite-gray"></div>

<div id = "dark-gray"></div>

<div id = "text-box">Text content here on the top of
the element stack - lower offset elements create a drop
shadow effect</div>
```

absolute-stack.css

```css
/* specify size of all div elements */
div    { width: 350px; height: 50px    }

/* specify position and color of each div element */

#text-box  { position: absolute; top: 20px; left: 20px;
             background: yellow; z-index: 4            }

#dark-gray { position: absolute; top: 24px; left: 24px;
             background: #666666; z-index: 3           }

#lite-gray { position: absolute; top: 28px; left: 28px;
             background: #999999; z-index: 2           }

#pale-gray { position: absolute; top: 32px; left: 32px;
             background: #CCCCCC; z-index: 1           }
```

A smaller offset creates a more convincing drop shadow effect – it is only large here to illustrate the contribution of each element to the shadow.

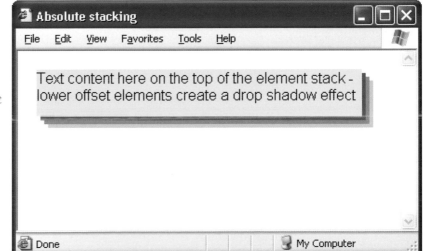

Positioning boxes relatively

In contrast to the absolute positioning scheme, which entirely removes an element from the normal flow layout, a relative positioning scheme adjusts the position of an element relative to the position it would originally occupy in the normal flow layout.

Changing from the static default positioning scheme, by assigning the relative value to the CSS position property, elements can be repositioned from their normal flow layout position using the offset properties top, right, bottom and left.

Notice how a negative value is assigned here – these can be used with other properties but may produce unexpected results.

For instance, specifying a top value of -15px moves the target element up and specifying a left value of 100px moves it to the right – but, crucially, the space occupied by its original layout position is preserved. Applying these relative position values to a span element target within a p paragraph element has this effect:

> a repositioned span target
> There is   on this line - it pays no
> heed to other paragraph content for it is a content box unto itself

Notice how the original content is shifted from its normal flow layout position into a newly-created content box positioned at the specified distance relative to its original position. This relative position will be maintained, even when the position of the outer containing element is changed.

So while absolute positioning may typically control the position of the outer element the relative positioning scheme is often useful to control the position of nested inner elements.

This can be used to enhance the previous example that created a drop-shadow effect on a block using several absolutely positioned elements. Creating further similar blocks using only absolute positioning would mean repeating style rules for each block, but controlling the position of subsidiary elements with relative positioning can provide greater flexibility.

The example opposite demonstrates this by creating classes in which style rules specify relative positions for the inner nested elements – so many blocks can easily use these classes for the drop shadow effect:

relative-positions.html

```html
<!-- complete block - repeated for second block -->
<div class = "pale-gray">
  <div class = "lite-gray">
    <div class = "dark-gray">
      <div class = "text-box">Text content here on the
      innermost element - outer offset elements create
      a drop shadow effect
      </div>
    </div>
  </div>
</div>
```

relative-positions.css

```css
/* specify size and color of outer (bottom) div */
.pale-gray { background: #CCCCCC; width: 350px;
             height: 50px; margin: 20px              }

/* specify offsets and colors of inner (higher) divs */
.lite-gray { background: #999999; position: relative;
             left: -4px; top: -4px; height: 100%      }

.dark-gray { background: #666666; position: relative;
             left: -4px; top: -4px; height: 100%      }

.text-box  { background: lime; position: relative;
             left: -4px; top: -4px; height: 100%      }
```

The margin property is only set on the outer element here to separate the two blocks in the normal flow layout.

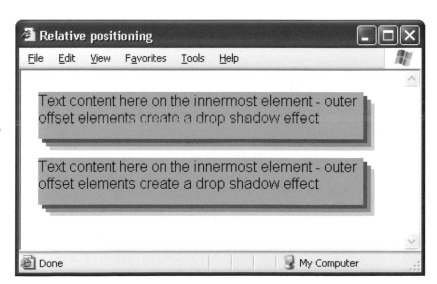

Fixing constant positions

A fixed positioning scheme, like the absolute positioning scheme, completely removes the target element's content box from the normal flow layout. But unlike absolute positioning, where offset values relate to the boundaries of the containing element, in fixed positioning the offset values relate to the viewport – the position is relative to the browser window, not to any part of the document.

At the time of writing Internet Explorer does not support fixed positioning. This example is shown here with the Firefox browser for completeness.

Usefully element positions can be fixed to emulate a frame-style interface where some frames remain at a constant position regardless of how the regular page content is scrolled. A typical frame-style interface might have a fixed navigation frame and a fixed header frame, like the interface in the following example. Style rules assign the CSS fixed keyword to the position property of the div elements representing the navigation and header frames. The offset properties top, right, bottom and left are used to fix their position so that only the div element containing the page content moves when the user scrolls this page.

fixed-positions.html

```
<!-- navigation "frame" panel -->
<div id = "menu">
<h2>Menu</h2><ul><li>item<li>item<li>item</ul></div>

<!-- header "frame" panel -->
<div id = "head"><h2>Header</h2></div>

<!-- page content "frame" panel -->
<div id = "main"><h2>Page content</h2>
<p><img src = "ruler.png"></p></div>
```

fixed-positions.css

```
/* set 100px-wide menu panel at top left full-height*/
#menu { position: fixed; top: 0; left: 0;
        width: 100px; height: 100%; background: aqua }

/* set 50px-high header panel at top beginning 100px
from left across to right edge - arranged uppermost */
#head { position: fixed; top: 0; left: 100px; right: 0;
        height: 50px; background: lime; z-index: 2   }

/* set main body at 100px from left and 50px from top
down to bottom edge - arranged lower back-to-front  */
#main { position: absolute; top: 50px; left: 100px;
        right: 0; bottom: 0; z-index: 1            }
```

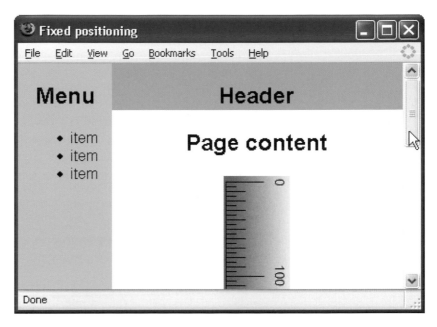

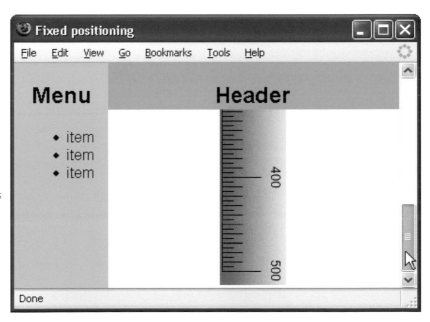

Fixed postioning is sometimes used to display an identity logo that remains visible at a constant position regardless of where the page is scrolled.

Floating content boxes

The CSS float property allows a content box to be positioned at the side boundary of its containing element – using the left or right keywords to specify the preferred side.

Unusually, floated content boxes are not truly removed from the normal flow layout but are repositioned within it. Space is not preserved at their original position but is, instead, filled with surrounding content which flows around the floated content box. Typically this feature is used to flow text around images which have been floated to the side of a containing paragraph element.

It is, however, possible to explicitly prevent text flowing alongside a floated content box using the CSS clear property – using the left, right, or both keyword to specify which side must be clear, otherwise the text will begin below the floated content box.

The following example uses the float property to position images at each side of the containing paragraph element. The text contained within the first two paragraphs flows around the floated content boxes but the third paragraph is targeted by a style rule using a clear constraint. This rule insists there should be no floating content to its left so the text is not allowed to flow around the image at its left but skips instead to begin below the image.

floating-positions.html

```
<p>Massive acceleration - the forbidden fruit. It's
easy to avoid such unlawful
<img class = "float-right" src = "viper-1.jpg">
activities in a normal vehicle. But there is an evil
serpent; a Viper, that tempts you to take a bite out of
the asphalt. With a tasty 500-hp V10 powering a mere
3,300-lb roadster, the Dodge Viper SRT-10 tricks you
into playing music with the loud pedal.</p>

<p>This car is too excessive, too epic for most people
to use on a daily basis.
<img class = "float-left" src = "viper-2.jpg">
But for otherwise nice couples who need only two seats
and a need to explore their darkest sins, this is the
car that will shame those who come up against them.</p>

<p class = "clear-left">If you can afford to... Buy
one. You need it. You'll like it.</p>
```

floating-positions.css

```css
/* show paragraph element content boxes */
p { background: yellow }

/* float to right boundary and show border */
.float-right { float: right; border: 3px dashed red    }

/* float to left boundary and show border */
.float-left  { float: left;  border: 3px dashed blue  }

/* ensure nothing is floating right of this element   */
.clear-right{ clear: right; background: aqua  }

/* ensure nothing is floating left of this element    */
.clear-left { clear: left; background: lime   }

/* ensure nothing is floating to the left or right    */
.clear-both { clear: both; background: orange }
```

Only the clear-left class has actually been applied in this example – apply the other clear classes to the paragraphs to see the effect they have.

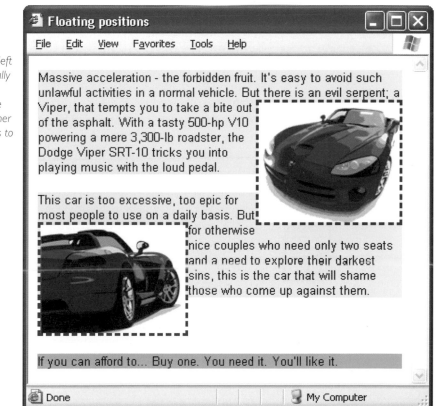

Clipping and handling overflow

Although CSS provides many controls to specify the precise position and size of content boxes there is no guarantee that their content will fit neatly within their boundaries in all circumstances. For instance, consider the effect of increasing the font size of text content that fits snugly within the boundaries of a block level box – the text will then bust out of the content box creating "overflow" outside its boundaries.

Overflowing content is generally visible by default, but the CSS overflow property can specify alternative handling behaviors using the hidden or scroll keywords.

Currently only rectangular shapes can be clipped – future specifications may allow other shapes to be clipped.

Conversely, the content within absolutely positioned block-level content boxes can be cropped using the clip property – the rectangular section to remain visible being identified by the coordinates of its corner points. In CSS these coordinates are assigned to the clip property as a space-separated list within the parentheses of a special rect() keyword, always in the order of top-left, top-right, bottom-right, bottom-left.

The following example has six div elements that each contain the same single image within their content box. The size of the content box in the first three div elements (100px x 100px) exactly matches the image size but the clip property values control which parts are visible. The size of the content box in the second three div elements (75px x 75px) is less than the image size so the overflow property values control how to handle the overflowing part of the image:

clip-and-overflow.html

```
<div class = "crop auto-clip"><img src = "p.png"></div>

<div class = "crop blok-clip"><img src = "p.png"></div>

<div class = "crop line-clip"><img src = "p.png"></div>

<div class = "spill show-overflow">
<img src = "p.png"></div>

<div class = "spill hide-overflow">
<img src = "p.png"></div>

<div class = "spill keep-overflow">
<img src = "p.png"></div>
```

clip-and-overflow.css

```
/* set top offset and div size */
div.crop       { position: absolute; top: 20px;
                 width: 100px; height: 100px        }

/* full image in 100px x 100px div */
div.auto-clip { left:  20px; clip: auto              }
/* crop to coordinates at top, right, bottom, left */
div.blok-clip { left: 140px;
                clip: rect(25px 100px 100px 25px)    }
div.line-clip { left: 260px;
                clip: rect(25px 100px 50px 0px)      }

/* set top offset and div size */
div.spill         { position: absolute; top: 150px;
                    width: 75px; height: 75px        }

/* full image in 75px x 75px div plus 25px overflow */
div.show-overflow  { left:  20px; overflow: visible  }
/* alternative handling for overflowing content */
div.hide-overflow  { left: 140px; overflow: hidden   }
div.keep-overflow  { left: 260px; overflow: scroll   }
```

The ability to toggle content visibility between visible and hidden presents exciting dynamic possibilities – see chapter 13 for more details.

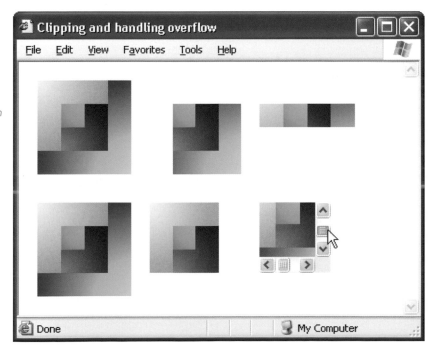

Summary

- In CSS the ability to center block-level element content boxes is provided by the **margin** property and the **auto** keyword

- Each element content box has a default **position** value of **static** in the normal layout positioning scheme

- Alternative positioning schemes can be specified by assigning the **absolute**, **relative**, or **fixed** keyword to the CSS **position** property

- The **absolute**, **relative** and **fixed** positioning schemes all use the offset properties **top**, **right**, **bottom**, and **left** to define positions

- An **absolute** positioning scheme places an element at the specified offset distances from the boundaries of its containing element

- A **relative** positioning scheme places an element at the specified offset distances from its position in the normal flow layout

- A **fixed** positioning scheme places an element at the specified offset distances from the edges of its containing viewport

- Both **absolute** and **fixed** positioning remove the element from the normal flow – but **relative** positioning preserves its original space

- Stack order can be explicitly specified by assigning integer values to the **z-index** property – the highest value appears uppermost

- The CSS **float** property can be assigned the **left** or **right** keyword to position a content box up to the side of its containing element

- Content can be prevented from flowing around floated boxes by assigning keywords **left**, **right** or **both** to the **clear** property

- Block-level content can be cropped by assigning a corner coordinate list as a **rect()** value to the CSS **clip** property

- The **overflow** property can specify how to handle overflowing block-level content with the **visible**, **hidden**, or **scroll** keywords

Laying out tables

This chapter begins by demonstrating how CSS can be used to control page layout – in place of a traditional HTML table layout. Examples illustrate how to style tables and how to assign table characteristics to XML elements for display in table format.

Covers

Chapter Ten

Controlling page layout

Traditionally web page authors have used HTML tables to control how page content is laid out by creating a borderless grid of cells into which components of the page are placed. This method works well enough for general layout but lacks the easy precise control offered by CSS. For instance, compare the ease at which elements can be absolutely positioned at specific coordinates with style rules to the difficulty of achieving the same with HTML tables. Unsurprisingly then, page layout with CSS is considered to be the superior layout method and web page authors are discouraged from continuing to use HTML tables for this purpose.

Moving to page layout with CSS invariably raises questions of how best to control the page content, so the following example suggests a CSS technique to create one of the most common page layouts of three column areas plus header and footer areas.

An image is included to this example, stretched to various dimensions, just to represent sample page content.

The HTML document simply lists five div elements for positioning with CSS – one for each required area. The first div element spans the page to create the header area. Below this are two div elements of specified width that are floated to the respective sides of the page to create the navigation and supplemental columns. A further div element is assigned side margin values, slightly greater than the width of each side column, to create a third central column for the main page content. The final div element is targeted by a style rule that assigns the both keyword to its clear property to ensure that the footer area will always appear, below the floating columns, at the end of the page.

page-layout.html

```
<div id = "hdr">Header panel
<br> <img src = "box.gif"> </div>

<div id = "nav">Navigational panel
<ul> <li>Link <li>Link </ul> </div>

<div id = "ads">Supplemental panel
<br> <img src = "box.gif"> </div>

<div id = "txt">Main page content panel
<br> <img src = "box.gif"> </div>

<div id = "ftr">Footer panel</div>
```

page-layout.css

```
/* set margins, padding, and inline-level alignment */
body,div { margin: 0; padding: 0; text-align: center }

/* set widths and float nav & ads div content boxes */
#nav        { float: left;  width: 100px        }
#ads        { float: right; width: 100px        }

/* set side txt margins 5px > nav & ads widths */
#txt        { margin-left: 105px; margin-right:105px }

/* ensure footer stays at the bottom */
#ftr        { clear: both }

/* show boundaries and set image sizes - for clarity */
#hdr, #ftr  { background: aqua                   }
#nav, #ads  { background: yellow                 }
#txt        { background: lime                   }

#hdr img { width: 250px; height:  25px }
#ads img { width:  75px; height: 100px }
#txt img { width: 150px; height: 200px }
```

The only fixed structural aspect in this example is the width of the navigation and supplemental panel – the height of all five components will increase to accommodate their content and the width of the header, main content, and footer panels will adjust to suit the window size.

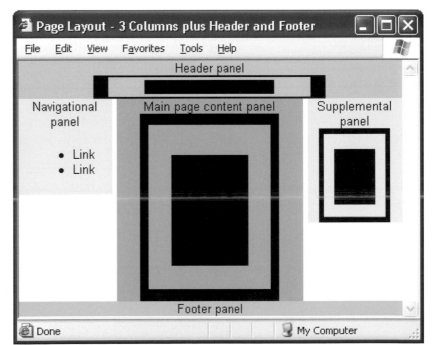

Sizing table columns

Although web page authors are now discouraged from using HTML tables for page layout, in favor of CSS, tables remain an invaluable format for the presentation of information within the content of a page.

When displaying an HTML table a web browser will, by default, automatically create a table layout sized to accommodate its content. This invariably produces a table with columns of varying widths where each column width is determined by the widest content of any cell in that column. This process requires the browser to examine the table content in some detail before it can compute the optimum table layout and, especially for large tables, can take some time before the browser is able to draw the table.

CSS provides an alternative which allows the browser to quickly compute a suitable table layout without examining the content of the entire table – a fixed-layout can be specified to the table-layout property of a table element with the fixed keyword.

Specify a first column width and a fixed layout rule to create a first column of custom width and all other columns of equal width to each other.

In a fixed layout the browser need only consider the width value of the table itself, and the width value of columns and cells on its first row to determine the table layout like this:

- The overall table width will be its specified width value or the sum of its column width values – whichever is the greater

- A specified column width value sets the width for that column

- When there is no specified column width value a specified cell width value sets the width for that column

- Any columns that have no specified width values, for either column or cell, will be sized equally within the table width

Different layouts can be seen in the example opposite which creates two table layouts for an identically-specified table width where no column or cell widths are specified. The default auto table-layout creates each column width according to its content, equalizing the space in each column. The fixed table-layout simply creates three columns of equal width.

Each table-layout style is identified by a caption – positioned above the table by a rule assigning a top value to its caption-side property.

table-layout.html

```
<table> <caption>Auto Layout</caption>
<tr>  <td>Text content</td>
      <td>Text content wider than 130px</td>
      <td>Text content</td>
</tr>
</table>

<table class = "fix"> <caption>Fixed Layout</caption>
<tr>  <td>Text content</td>
      <td>Text content wider than 130px</td>
      <td>Text content</td>
</tr>
</table>
```

CSS

table-layout.html

```
/* show boundaries */
table { border: 3px dashed blue; text-align: center }
td    { border: 3px solid red; background: yellow    }
caption        { background: aqua            }

/* set table width, caption position and margin */
table          { width: 390px ; caption-side: top;
                 margin-bottom: 20px        }

/* compute column widths regardless of cell content */
table.fix      { table-layout: fixed        }
```

The caption-side property can alternatively specify a "bottom" value – but the actual treatment of captions is browser-specific.

Table layout
File Edit View Favorites Tools Help
Auto Layout
Text content	Text content wider than 130px	Text content
Fixed Layout
Text content	Text content wider than 130px	Text content
Done   My Computer

Spacing table cells

The distance between table cell borders can be specified as a unit value assigned to the CSS border-spacing property. This easily allows cells to be spread some distance apart throughout a table.

A single specified border-spacing value will be applied uniformly to all cell separations – in much the same way as with the HTML cellspacing attribute.

CSS provides greater flexibility by allowing two values to be assigned to the border-spacing property as a space-separated list. The first will be applied to the horizontal spacing, at the left and right of each table cell, and the second will be applied to the vertical spacing, at the top and bottom of each table cell. This means that different distances can be specified for the horizontal and vertical cell spacing throughout a table.

Another possibility offered by CSS is the ability to hide table cells which contain no content. These frequently occur due to the grid format of tables which does not always conveniently match the number of cells required. For instance, displaying nine content items in a table of five rows and two columns.

Creating a style rule with the CSS empty-cells property assigned a hide value will cause the browser to not display the border and background of any cell that contains absolutely no content. Cells that contain any content at all, even if it's simply a   non-breaking space entity, will still be visible.

Conversely, a rule can explicitly specify that empty cells should be displayed by assigning a show value to the empty-cells property.

Empty table cells that are hidden do continue to have a presence in the table layout inasmuch as their border-spacing values are preserved. This can be witnessed in the example opposite that sets a uniform border-spacing of 20px throughout a table, and sets its empty-cells property to hide. Although the center cell gets hidden its presence is evident by the border-spacing between the other two cells – 40px apart rather than just 20px that would appear if the hidden cell did not exist.

spacing-and-hiding.html

```
<table>
<tr>
<td>1</td> <td></td> <td>3</td>
</tr>
</table>

<table class = "space">
<tr>
<td>1</td> <td></td> <td>3</td>
</tr>
</table>
```

spacing-and hiding.hcss

```
/* add border spacing and hide empty cells */
table.space { border-spacing: 20px;
              empty-cells: hide                         }

/* show boundaries */
table       { width: 350px; margin: 20px;
              border: 3px dotted red                    }

td     { border: 3px solid blue; background: aqua      }
```

This example is illustrated with the Firefox web browser – the appearance may vary with Internet Explorer.

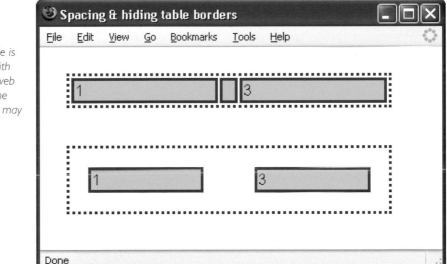

Collapsing table borders

The borders of adjacent table borders, and table cell borders, can be made to "collapse" into a single border by assigning the collapse keyword to the CSS border-collapse property. This requires the browser to perform a series of evaluations, comparing the existing borders, to determine how the collapsed border should appear:

- Visibility evaluation: where one of the borders to be collapsed has a border-style value of hidden that value takes precedence – so the collapsed border at that location will be hidden

The separate keyword can be assigned to the border-collapse property to explicitly prevent collapsing borders.

- Width evaluation: where two visible borders with different border-width values are to be collapsed the highest value takes precedence – so the collapsed border will be the greater width

- Style evaluation: where two visible borders of equal width are to be collapsed their border-style value sets the precedence in the descending status order of double, solid, dashed, dotted, ridge, outset, groove, inset – so the collapsed border at that location will be in the style of highest status. For instance, a double styles wins out over a solid style

- Color evaluation: where two visible borders of equal width and identical style are to be collapsed the border-color value is determined in the descending status order of cell, row, row group, column, column group, table – so that collapsed border will be in the color of highest status, For instance, the cell border-color value wins out over the table border-color value

At the time of writing Internet Explorer does not accurately support border collapsing. This example is shown here with the Firefox browser for completeness.

The effect of collapsing table borders can be seen in the example opposite which collapses both table and cell borders. Here the width evaluation, between the table border-width and the cells border-width value determines the collapsed border-width will be 5px (5px wins out over 2px).

In comparing the adjacent border-style values between the first and second cells the style evaluation determines the collapsed border-style will be double (double wins out over dotted).

Similarly, comparing the adjacent border-style values between the second and third cells the style evaluation determines the collapsed border-style will be solid (solid wins out over dotted).

collapsing-borders.html

```
<table>
<tr>  <td class = "twin">1</td>
      <td class = "dots">2</td>
      <td class = "full">3</td>
</tr>
</table>

<table class = "fold">
<tr>  <td class = "twin">1</td>
      <td class = "dots">2</td>
      <td class = "full">3</td>
</tr>
</table>
```

collapsing-borders.css

```
/* set table size and margin size */
table { width: 350px; height: 60px; margin: 20px     }

/* set borders to collapse */
table.fold  { border-collapse: collapse              }

/* set borders */
table       { border: 2px solid black  }
td.twin     { border: 5px double green }
td.full     { border: 5px solid blue   }
td.dots     { border: 5px dotted red   }
```

This example is illustrated with the Firefox web browser – the appearance may vary with Internet Explorer.

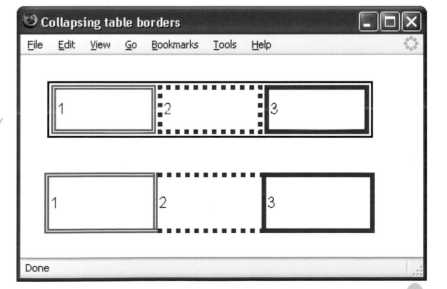

Assigning table characteristics

The CSS display property can accept a range of values to specify that a target element should be treated as a table component – emulating the default behavior of HTML tags that a browser automatically recognizes for table components.

HTML tag	CSS equivalent	HTML tag	CSS equivalent
<table>	table	<col>	table-column
<tr>	table-row	<colgroup>	table-column-group
<thead>	table-header-group	<th>	table-cell
<tbody>	table-row-group	<td>	
<tfoot>	table-footer-group	<caption>	table-caption

The CSS values which can be used with the display property to assign table characteristics are listed above, together with the HTML tag they most closely represent. The following example demonstrates how they may be used to assign table characteristics to target elements of an XML document:

xml-table.xml

```
<?xml version = "1.0" encoding = "UTF-8" ?>
<?xml-stylesheet
       href = "xml-table.css" type = "text/css" ?>

<liga>
 <cap>La Liga Top 3</cap>
 <hdrs>
  <lbl>Position</lbl> <lbl>Team</lbl> <lbl>Points</lbl>
 </hdrs>
 <rows>
  <team>
   <pos>1</pos> <name>Barcelona</name> <pts>84</pts>
  </team>
  <team>
   <pos>2</pos> <name>Real Madrid</name> <pts>80</pts>
  </team>
  <team>
   <pos>3</pos> <name>Villareal</name> <pts>65</pts>
  </team>
 </rows>
</liga>
```

The web browser only knows to display these elements in table format because of the CSS style rules.

...cont'd

xml-table.css

```
/*  assign table characteristics to XML tags... */

liga                { display: table                }

hdrs                { display: table-header-group   }

rows                { display: table-row-group      }

team                { display: table-row            }

name,pos,pts,lbl    { display: table-cell           }

cap                 { display: table-caption        }

/* now apply styles... center the table, add top
margin, set width, border spacing & border */
liga { margin: auto; margin-top: 20px;
       width: 300px; border-spacing: 3px;
       border: 8px ridge lime                        }

/* set header and row backgrounds */
hdrs { background: lime  }
rows { background: aqua  }
```

This example is illustrated with the Firefox web browser – the appearance may vary with Internet Explorer.

Mozilla Firefox

File Edit View Go Bookmarks Tools Help

La Liga Top 3

Position	Team	Points
1	Barcelona	84
2	Real Madrid	80
3	Villareal	65

Done

Summary

- Page layout with CSS is considered to be the superior layout method – web page authors are discouraged from continuing to use HTML tables for this purpose

- The default table-layout value of auto will create a table with column widths to suit the widest content of any cell in the column

- A fixed table-layout quickly creates a table from the table width value and the width value of columns and cells on its first row

- The caption-side property can be assigned values of top or bottom to specify the location of a table caption

- A unit value can be assigned to the CSS border-spacing property to specify a uniform distance at which cells should be spaced

- The border-spacing property can be assigned two unit values in a single rule to specify horizontal and vertical spacing between cells

- The empty-cells property can be assigned values of hide or show to specify whether empty table cells should appear

- Adjacent table borders can be collapsed into a single border by assigning the collapse keyword to the border-collapse property

- The appearance of a collapsed border is determined by comparing the visibility, width, style, and color of the borders that are to be collapsed

- Table characteristics can be assigned to a target element using the CSS display property

- Keywords table, table-row, table-header-group, table-row-group, table-footer-group, table-column, table-column-group, table-caption and table-cell emulate HTML table component elements

Formatting lists and backgrounds

This chapter describes, by example, how CSS style rules can specify how lists should appear. It also demonstrates how they can apply backgrounds to elements of an HTML document.

Covers

Chapter Eleven

Electing marker styles

A list "marker" indicates the beginning of an item in a list –typically a bullet in an unordered <ul> list, and an incrementing number or letter in an <ol> ordered list. The browser conducts in item count in each case but usually only uses this to number the items in an ordered list display.

The CSS list-style-type property can specify an alternative type of marker for any list – so unordered lists can have numbered markers and ordered lists can have bullets, if so desired.

Keywords allow the bullet marker type to be specified as disc, circle, or square, and number marker type as lower-roman, upper-roman, decimal, or decimal-leading-zero.

Alphabetical marker types can be specified with the lower-latin, upper-latin, and lower-greek keywords. Additionally the specifications provide keywords for other alphabets, such as armenian and georgian, but a suitable font is needed for the marker to be displayed correctly by the web browser.

The list-style-type property can also be assigned the none keyword to explicitly suppress the markers so they will not be displayed – they do remain in the item count however.

Each of the common list marker types appears in this example:

Both numerical markers and alphabetical markers display the incrementing item count.

list-style-types.html

```
<h3>Alphabetical list marker types:</h3>
<ol id = "list-0">lower-latin<li>...<li>...<li>...</ol>
<ol id = "list-1">upper-latin<li>...<li>...<li>...</ol>
<ol id = "list-2">lower-greek<li>...<li>...<li>...</ol>

<h3>Bullet list marker types:</h3>
<ol id = "list-3">disc<li>...<li>...<li>...</ol>
<ol id = "list-4">circle<li>...<li>...<li>...</ol>
<ol id = "list-5">square<li>...<li>...<li>...</ol>

<h3>Numerical list marker types:</h3>
<ol id = "list-6">lower-roman<li>...<li>...<li>...</ol>
<ol id = "list-7">upper-roman<li>...<li>...<li>...</ol>
<ol id = "list-8">decimal<li>...<li>...<li>...</ol>
<ol id = "list-9">decimal-leading-zero
<li>...<li>...<li>...</ol>
```

list-style-types.css

```
/* alphabetical marker lists... */
#list-0      { list-style-type: lower-latin    }
#list-1      { list-style-type: upper-latin    }
#list-2      { list-style-type: lower-greek    }
/* bullet marker lists... */
#list-3      { list-style-type: disc      }
#list-4      { list-style-type: circle  }
#list-5      { list-style-type: square  }
/* numerical marker lists */
#list-6      { list-style-type: lower-roman    }
#list-7      { list-style-type: upper-roman    }
#list-8      { list-style-type: decimal        }
#list-9      { list-style-type: decimal-leading-zero }
```

This example is illustrated with the Firefox web browser – the appearance may vary with Internet Explorer.

List marker types

File   Edit   View   Go   Bookmarks   Tools   Help

Alphabetical list marker types:

lower-latin	upper-latin	lower-greek
a. ...	A. ...	α. ...
b. ...	B. ...	β. ...
c. ...	C. ...	γ. ...

Bullet list marker types:

disc	circle	square
◆ ...	◇ ...	■ ...
◆ ...	◇ ...	■ ...
◆ ...	◇ ...	■ ...

Numerical list marker types:

lower-roman	upper-roman	decimal
i. ...	I. ...	1. ...
ii. ...	II. ...	2. ...
iii. ...	III. ...	3. ...

decimal-leading-zero
01. ...
02. ...
03. ...

Done

Assigning a graphic marker

Optionally an image may be used as a list marker, in place of the standard marker types, using the CSS list-style-image property. The image to be used as the marker is assigned to this property via the special url() keyword which should state its file name, and path if applicable, between the parentheses.

Always specify alternative marker bullets for when the images cannot be used.

If the image is not located the browser will display the default marker type – or that specified to its list-style-type property.

The simple example below displays an appropriate image marker for each list item and also specifies different marker bullet types to be used where the images cannot be located:

list-style-images.html

```
<ol>
<li class = "tick">Do maximize menu item hit areas
<li class = "tick">Do use the img tag's alt attribute
<li class = "tick">Do include a link title attribute
<li class = "nono">Don't use images for menus
<li class = "nono">Don't rely on a logo for a home link
<li class = "nono">Don't use frames for page layout
</ol>
```

list-style-images.html

```
.tick {       list-style-image: url(tick.gif);
              list-style-type: disc; color: green    }

.nono {       list-style-image: url(cross.gif);
              list-style-type: square; color: red    }
```

Positioning list markers

In considering the box model used to display lists the browser creates a block-level content box for the entire list and inline content boxes for each list item. Typically a left-margin insets the list item content boxes and each marker appears up against the right edge of this margin area – outside the list item content box.

The position of the marker may be explicitly specified using the CSS list-style-position property and inside or outside keywords.

The example below shows item markers both outside the list item content boxes (the default behavior) and inside them:

list-style-positions.html

```
<ol id = "outside-markers">
<li>List<li>Markers<li>Outside content box
</ol>

<ol id =  "inside-markers">
<li>List<li>Markers<li>Inside content box
</ol>
```

list-style-positions.css

```
/* set marker positions */
#outside-markers    { list-style-position: outside    }

#inside-markers     { list-style-position: inside     }

/* show boundaries */
li     { background: lime   }
```

Notice that the margin area is the same in each case.

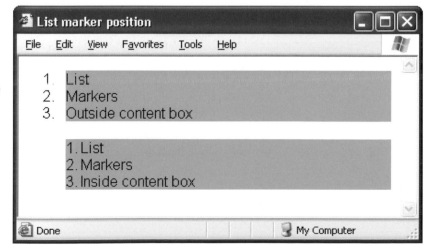

Using the list shorthand

The ability to control list item marker styles with the CSS list-style-type, list-style-image, and list-style-position properties may be combined using the list-style shorthand property.

This can be assigned a value for each separate property, as a space separated list, and they may be listed in any order, such as:

```
list-style {
list-style-image list-style-type list-style-position }
```

or

```
list-style {
list-style-type list-style-position list-style-image }
```

Inner nested lists can inherit their marker styles from the outer list – explicitly specify an alternative or use the none keyword to suppress markers.

Any one, or two, of the three property values may be omitted – they will be automatically replaced by their default value. For instance:

```
list-style { list-style-image }
```

explicitly specifies an image to be used as the marker but infers default list-style-type (disc) and default list-style-position (outside).

This example uses both list-style and border shorthand style rules to specify the appearance of nested list items:

list-shorthand.html

```
<ol id = "outer-list">
<li>Green list
      <ol id =  "inner-list">
      <li>Blue list
            <ul id =  "inmost-list">
            <li>Red list
            <li>Marker
            <li>Outside content box
            </ul>
      <li>Markers
      <li>Inside content box
      </ol>
<li>Markers
<li>Inside content box
</ol>
```

list-shorthand.css

```
/* set marker type, position, and image */

#outer-list {
        list-style: url(lilguy.gif) disc inside;
        border: 2px dashed green                    }

#inner-list {
        list-style: square inside;
        border: 2px dashed blue                     }

#inmost-list {
        list-style: upper-roman outside;
        border: 2px dashed red                      }

/* show boundaries */
#outer-list li    { background: lime;   color: green }

#inner-list li    { background: aqua;   color: blue  }

#inmost-list li   { background: yellow; color: red   }
```

This example is illustrated with the Firefox web browser – the appearance may vary with Internet Explorer.

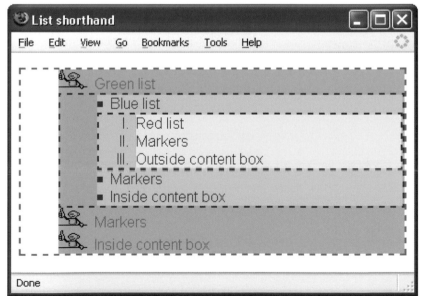

Choosing backgrounds

The background color of any target element can be specified by assigning a valid color value (as described on page 48) to the CSS background-color property.

Notice that the "background" property is used to assign colors in the examples listed in this book – not the "background-color" property. This is done to keep the sample code concise but "background" is actually a shorthand property (see page 144).

Additionally, a background image can be specified for any target element using the background-image property. The image is assigned using the special url() keyword – stating its file name, and path if applicable, between the parentheses.

When the specified image is located it is placed at the top left corner of the target element's background. The default behavior of the browser's background-repeat property is set to repeat the image, tiling it row by row across the entire element background.

The tiling behavior can be changed, however, by assigning a different value to the background-repeat property using the keywords repeat-x, repeat-y, or no-repeat.

Using the repeat-x and repeat-y values restricts the tiling to a single line of background images, tiled along the x or y axis. In each case the browser begins by placing the specified image in the top left corner of that target element's background. With the repeat-x value the image is then tiled in a single row, from left to right, whereas with the repeat-y value the image is then tiled in a single column, from top to bottom.

Logically enough the no-repeat value will prevent the image being tiled at all – a single image version of the image appears alone at the top left of the element's background.

Background images are placed on a layer above the background's color layer so using an image with transparent areas will allow the background color to shine through. This can be seen in the example opposite that specifies a background-color value for each div element with the fuchsia color keyword.

The default repeat tiling effect is seen in the top div element background but style rules use the background-repeat property to control how the background image appears in the other div elements. Also a separate background-color value is specified for the h2 heading element within each div element.

background-repeat.html

background-repeat.css

```
<div>              <br>  <h2>repeat (default)</h2> </div>

<div class = "bg-x">     <br>   <h2>repeat-x</h2> </div>
<div class = "bg-y">     <br>   <h2>repeat-y</h2> </div>
<div class = "bg-one"> <br> <h2>no-repeat</h2>  </div>
```

```
h2     { padding: 2px; display: inline          }
div    { width: 352px; height: 64px;
         margin: 15px; text-align: center        }

/* set background colors, image and repeat */
h2              { background-color: yellow        }
div             { background-color: fuchsia       }
div             { background-image: url(tile.gif) }
.bg-x           { background-repeat: repeat-x     }
.bg-y           { background-repeat: repeat-y     }
.bg-one         { background-repeat: no-repeat    }
```

tile.gif – the red areas are transparent.

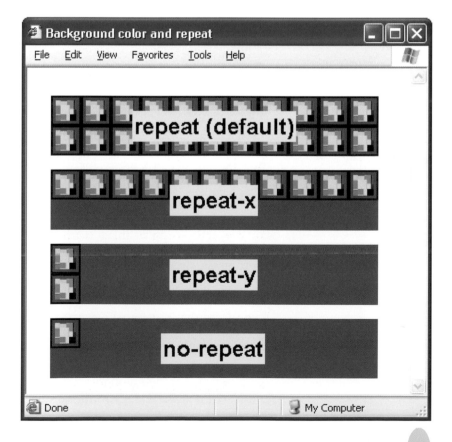

Positioning background images

The position of an original background image can be changed from the default position, at the top left corner of the target element's background, using the background-position property and the keywords left, center, right, top, and bottom.

The background-position property can be assigned two keywords to specify the location. For instance, the image could be placed in the bottom right corner. Alternatively it can be assigned just one keyword and will assume the second value to be center – specifying top puts the image at the top center of the background.

The background-position property may also be assigned percentage values to specify the position with greater precision. Their values specify the location with these equivalents to the keywords:

x-axis			y-axis
			top (0%)
left (0%)	center (50%)	right (100%)	center (50%)
			bottom (100%)

The background-position property can also accept unit values to specify an offset position of the top left corner of the image from the top left corner of the element. But this is only useful where the element size cannot change – use keywords or percentage values for greater flexibility.

The keyword values may be specified in any order but percentages must be in order of x-axis value, then y-axis value. As with keywords, where only one percentage value is specified the second will be assumed to be center (50%).

Interestingly, when computing the image position with percentages the browser first identifies a point within the image at the specified coordinates, then places that point at the same coordinates within the target element. For instance, with values of 50% 50% the browser first identifies a point at the exact center of the image, then places that point at the exact center of the target element.

In this example, demonstrating background-position control, the rule specifying percentage values of 20% 50% takes a point within the image that is 20% along its x-axis, and 50% down its y-axis, and places it at the same coordinates within the target element.

background-position.html

background-position.css

```
<div> <br> <h2>top left (default)</h2> </div>

<div class = "bg-btm"><br><h2>bottom left</h2>   </div>
<div class = "bg-ctr"><br><h2>[ center] right</h2></div>
<div class = "bg-qtr"><br><h2>20% 50%</h2>        </div>
```

```
h2      { background-color: yellow; padding: 2px;
                display: inline                      }
div    { background-color: fuchsia;      width: 352px;
           background-image: url(tile.gif); height: 64px;
           background-repeat: no-repeat;   margin: 15px;
           text-align: center                        }

/* background position classes... */
.bg-btm      { background-position: bottom left      }
.bg-ctr      { background-position: right            }
.bg-qtr      { background-position: 20% 50%          }
```

The background-position values set the position of the original background image within the target element – tiling can begin from that position by adding a background-repeat rule.

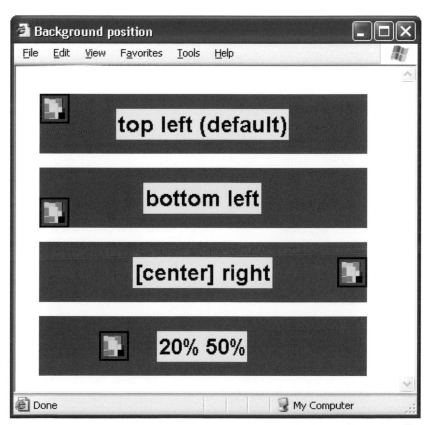

Using the background shorthand

Typically a background image will move with all other contents, when a user scrolls the windows up or down, as the CSS background-attachment property has a scroll value by default. This behavior can be changed by assigning a fixed value so the background image will remain at its specified coordinates relative to the viewport - useful to keep in constant view a background logo image regardless of how the window is scrolled.

Remember that the background shorthand applies default values for those properties not explicitly specified, not no value – the default values may overwrite previous values.

All the CSS background properties of background-attachment, background-position, background-repeat, background-image, and background-color, can be specified together in a single rule using the CSS background shorthand property. This can accept one or more valid values stated, in any order, as a space-separated list – the only restriction being that where two values are specified for the background-position property they must appear together.

The background shorthand property assumes the default value for any background properties that are not explicitly specified – so the following style rules have the same effect:

```
background: white url(tile.gif)
background: white url(tile.gif) top left repeat scroll
```

In the following example the background shorthand property specifies that a background image should be tiled along a single row across the center of the target body element and its position fixed relative to the viewport. This means that the h2 heading element, and img image element, move when the user scrolls the page but the background image remains constantly in view:

background-shorthand.css

```
h2      { padding: 2px; background: yellow }

/*      set body background properties as...
        background-color: fuchsia
        background-image: url(tile.gif)
        background-repeat: repeat-x
        background-position: center
        background-attachment: fixed        ... */
body {
background: fuchsia url(tile.gif) repeat-x center fixed
}
```

```html
<body>
    <h2>fixed</h2>
    <img src = "ruler.png">
</body>
```

background-shorthand.html

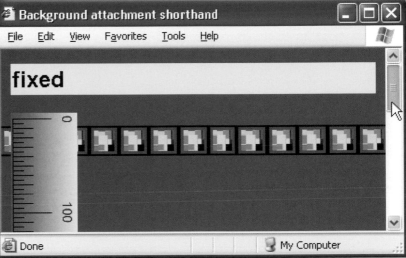

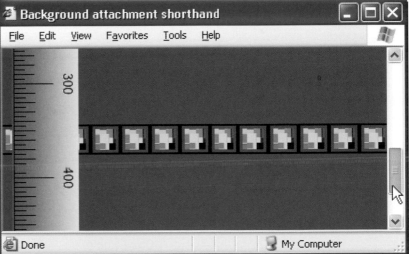

Summary

- The CSS list-style-type property can specify a bullet marker type using the keywords disc, circle, and square – or a numerical marker type using the keywords decimal, decimal-leading-zero, lower-roman, and upper-roman

- Alternatively the list-style-type property can specify an alphabetical marker type using the keywords lower-latin, upper-latin, and lower-greek, or other alphabets such as armenian and georgian

- An image can be specified as a graphical marker to the CSS list-style-image property using the special url() keyword

- The list-style-position property can be assigned the keywords inside or outside to determine whether, or not, the list markers should appear inside the list item content box

- All list property values can be specified in a single rule as a space-separated list to the CSS list-style shorthand property

- The background-color property can be assigned any valid color value to specify the background color of a target element

- A background image can be specified to the CSS background-image property using the special url() keyword

- The background-repeat property can be assigned keywords repeat-x, repeat-y, repeat or no-repeat to control tiling

- An initial background image position can be specified to the background-position property using the keywords left, center, right, top, and bottom , or as percentage values, or as unit values

- When only one value is assigned to the background-position property the second value is assumed to be center (50%)

- All background property values can be specified in a single rule as a space-separated list to the CSS background shorthand property

Generating content

This chapter demonstrates how CSS pseudo-classes and pseudo elements can enhance the appearance of a document. It also illustrates automatic numbering, cursor customization, and outlining content.

Covers

Chapter Twelve

Enhancing text

CSS provides four pseudo elements, :before, :after, :first-letter, and :first-line, that can be included in the style rule selector to enhance the actual content of the target element.

The :before and :after pseudo elements place generated content around the original content and appear in the selector immediately after the target. For instance, a selector p:before could be used to generate content before the content of each paragraph element.

The :before and :after pseudo elements generate enhancements around the original content using the special CSS content property to specify the additional content to be generated.

Most simply, the content property can be assigned text, enclosed within quotes, to specify a text string to be generated. In this case spaces within the text string will be preserved in the generated content.

Alternatively, the content property may be assigned the keywords open-quote or close-quote to generate quotes around the original content.

Generated content is not limited to text strings as the special url() keyword can be used with the content property to specify non-textual content to be generated. For instance, an image might be specified using url(image.png) to generate the image.

Additionally, the special attr() keyword can be used with the content property to specify an attribute name of the target element whose value should appear as generated content. For instance, an attribute might be specified using url(src) to generate the value of the src attribute in the target element.

Multiple items to be generated can be assigned to the content property as a space-separated list, mixing any of the above. This feature is used in the example opposite to add both text strings and an attribute value to the targeted a element in the final paragraph. All original paragraph element content here is preceded and followed by generated content and the hyperlinks receive a variety of generated enhancements:

before-after.html

```
<p>Get more <a href = "info.pdf">info</a> here</p>
<p>Get more
<a href = "info.pdf" class = "quo">info</a> here</p>
<p>Get more
<a href = "info.pdf" class = "lnk">info</a> here</p>
<p>Get more
<a href = "info.pdf" class = "pdf">info</a> here</p>
<p>Get more
<a href = "info.pdf" class = "att">info</a> here</p>
```

before-after.css

```
/* insert string items before and after paragraphs */
p:before { content: "*..."; background: yellow      }
p:after  { content: "...!" ; background: aqua        }

/* insert red quotes before and after target */
a[href].quo:before { content: open-quote;  color: red }
a[href].quo:after  { content: close-quote; color: red }

/* insert orange string before hyperlinks */
a[href].lnk:before { content: "[link]: "; color: orange}

/* insert image and attribute value after hyperlinks */
a[href].pdf:after  { content: url(pdf-ico.gif)        }
a[href].att:after  { content: " [" attr(href) "] ";
                     color: green                      }
```

Generated content is added inside the content block of the target element – so the enhancements to these hyperlinks are part of the link.

This example is illustrated with the Firefox web browser – the appearance may vary with Internet Explorer.

Pseudo Elements :before and :after

File Edit View Go Bookmarks Tools Help

*...Get more <u>info</u> here...!

*...Get more <u>"info"</u> here...!

*...Get more <u>[link]: info</u> here...!

*...Get more <u>info</u> 📄 here...!

*...Get more <u>info [info.pdf]</u> here...!

Done

Numbering sections

The :before pseudo element, introduced in the previous example, can insert generated content to automatically number sections of an HTML document using the special CSS counter() keyword. This specifies the name of a counter, within its parentheses, to insert the current value of that counter.

A counter to count the instances of a target in an HTML document must first be created by assigning a chosen name and an incremental value as a space-separated list to the CSS counter-increment property.

Notice that the generated content in this example includes text space for formatting purposes.

The counter will begin counting from zero by default and will increment by the specified incremental value for every instance of the target. Optionally, the explicitly specified incremental value may be omitted from the rule and the value of 1 will be assumed. For example, counter-increment:num creates a counter called "num" that will start counting from zero, and increment by one.

Additionally, the counter can be made to start counting from a number other than zero by assigning the chosen name and an explicit initial value as a space-separated list to the CSS counter-reset property.

Once a counter has been created its current value can be inserted before the target as generated content in a CSS pseudo element.

In the following example a counter named "num" is created to count the number of instances of h2 heading elements and a counter named "sub" is created to count the number of instances of h3 heading elements. The :before pseudo element inserts the counter value before each heading – the current num counter value before each h2 topic heading, the current value of both num and sub counters before each h3 section heading.

The first h3 element in the second topic contains a class attribute that is targeted by a rule to reset the sub counter to zero. Counting once more from zero, the first element in the second topic again increments the counter to 1, the second to 2, and so on:

counter.html

```
<h2>Topic</h2>
<h3>Section</h3> <h3>Section</h3> <h3>Section</h3>

<h2>Topic</h2>
<h3 class = "start">Section</h3>
<h3>Section</h3> <h3>Section</h3>
```

counter.css

```
/* create "num" and "sub" counters to increment by 1 */
h2      { counter-increment: num 1                        }
h3      { counter-increment: sub 1; text-indent: 10%    }

/* insert topic counter values */
h2:before { content: counter(num) " " ;
                background: aqua                           }

/* insert topic and section counter values */
h3:before { content: counter(num) "." counter(sub) " ";
                background: lime                           }

/* reset the "sub" counter to zero */
h3.start  { counter-reset: sub 0                          }
```

This example is illustrated with the Opera web browser – the appearance may vary with Internet Explorer.

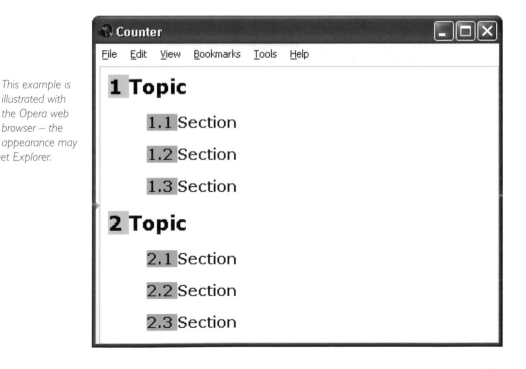

Highlighting content

Like the :before and :after pseudo elements the :first-letter and :first-line pseudo elements effectively insert imaginary elements to enhance the actual document content.

The :first-letter pseudo element styles the very first letter within a block-level target element. Typically this is useful to highlight the initial letter of each paragraph in a document.

Similarly the :first-line pseudo element styles the very first line of text within a block-level element and is useful to highlight the first line of each paragraph within a document. The extent of the first line is recalculated if the element gets resized – if the user resizes the window the style is applied to the current first line content.

Note that the :first-letter and :first-line pseudo elements cannot be used to style inline-level elements, such as hyperlinks.

In addition to the four pseudo elements CSS also provides a number of pseudo-classes that can be included with the selector in a style rule. The :first-child and :lang() pseudo-classes are typically used to highlight content, much like the pseudo elements above.

It is important to recognize that the :first-child pseudo-class styles the target element that is the first child within an outer element – not the first child of the target element. So in the example opposite the :first-child pseudo-class styles only the first span element within each p element parent paragraph.

Notice that quotes are not needed around the two-letter language identifier with the :lang() pseudo-class – simpler syntax and greater power make this method preferable to the attribute selector method for languages.

The :lang() pseudo-class can be included in a style rule selector to target an element by its language as an alternative to using the attribute selector method introduced on page 29. For instance, the selector *:lang(es) in the example is equivalent to *[lang | = "es"]. Both target all elements with Spanish language content but the :lang() pseudo-class is the more powerful method as it considers more than just the HTML element's lang attribute to determine the content language – utilizing document headers and meta data.

Unlike pseudo elements, multiple pseudo-classes can be included in a single selector. For instance p:first-child:lang(fr) would target the paragraph that is the first child of an outer element and of French language content.

first.html

```
<p>In what was once Texcoco lake, birthplace of
<span>pre-Hispanic civilizations</span>
, lies the
<span lang = "es">Ciudad de los Palacios</span>
(City of Palaces) that is today, Mexico City.
</p>

<p>Mexico City offers visitors a great many different
interesting sites to visit, from
<span>pre-Columbian Mexico</span>
to modern and
<span>cosmopolitan 21st century Mexico</span>.
</p>
```

first.css

```
/* style the first letter of each paragraph */
p:first-letter     { font-size: 200%; color: red     }

/* style the first line of each paragraph */
p:first-line       { background-color: yellow         }

/* style the first span in each paragraph */
span:first-child   { background-color: aqua           }

/* style all Spanish content */
*:lang(es)         { background-color: lime            }
```

Pseudo :first-letter :first-line :lang :first-child

File   Edit   View   Favorites   Tools   Help

In what was once Texcoco lake, birthplace of pre-Hispanic civilizations, lies the Ciudad de los Palacios (City of Palaces) that is today, Mexico City.

Mexico City offers visitors a great many different interesting sites to visit, from pre-Columbian Mexico to modern and cosmopolitan 21st century Mexico.

Done   My Computer

Customizing cursors

The CSS cursor property can specify the type of cursor icon that should be displayed when the pointer hovers over a target element. Its default value of auto allows the browser to determine which cursor icon to display but explicitly assigning the default keyword to the cursor property forces the browser to use the operating system's default cursor icon.

Alternative cursor keywords, together with the cursor icons they typically represent in Windows, are listed in this table.

By default Windows uses the same resize icon for each diagonal (north-south, etc) but these can be individually different icons.

Keyword	Cursor	Keyword	Cursor
default		n-resize	
pointer		ne-resize	
crosshair		e-resize	
move		se-resize	
text		s-resize	
wait		sw-resize	
progress		w-resize	
help		nw-resize	

Traditionally, with HTML documents, the pointer cursor indicates a hyperlink, the move cursor indicates a item that can be dragged, and the text cursor indicates a component in which text can be selected. As most users are familiar with these cursor conventions it is best to adhere to them.

The wait cursor means that the user should not proceed until the current task has completed, whereas the progress cursor means the user can proceed while the program continues to complete the task.

In addition to system cursors the CSS cursor property may also specify an image for use as a custom cursor using the special url() keyword to state its file name and path. Multiple images can be assigned as a comma-separated list of url() values but each list should end with a regular cursor keyword to specify which cursor to use if none of the specified images can be located.

In this example the system help cursor icon is specified to the cursor property, to be displayed when the pointer hovers over the first paragraph element. A specified custom image file redaro.cur is assigned with the url() keyword to be displayed when the pointer hovers over the second paragraph – or the default system cursor icon is to be used when that image cannot be found.

cursor.html

```html
<p class = "help-cursor">Browser defined help cursor</p>

<p class = "arrow-cursor">
Custom arrow cursor (or browser default)</p>
```

cursor.css

```css
/* show boundaries */
p       { border: 1px solid black;
          height: 50px; background: yellow            }

/* set cursors... */
p.help-cursor  { cursor: help }
p.arrow-cursor { cursor: url(redaro.cur), default     }
```

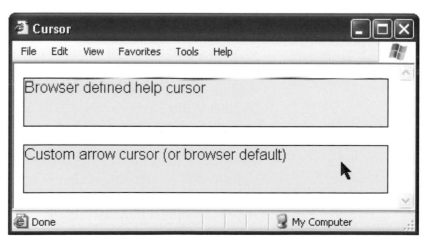

Outlining components

Components of an HTML document can be emphasized using the CSS outline property to outline target content. Unusually, an outline is drawn around the content of the target element on a layer above the content box – so it does not influence the box model in any way.

The outline shorthand property is similar to the border shorthand property inasmuch as it can accept very nearly all of the same values to specify style, width, and color, as a space-separated list.

The specifications do not define how multiple overlapping outlines are drawn, or how outlines are drawn for boxes that are partially obscured behind other elements.

As with the border property a style must always be explicitly specified to the outline property but the width and color values may be omitted. There are also outline-style, outline-width and outline-color properties to specify individual values.

Unlike borders, outlines have a uniform style on all sides – so there are no outline properties to specify individual side values, nor can the outline-style property have a hidden value.

In addition to specifying color in the usual way the outline-color property can be assigned the invert keyword to have the browser select a color that contrasts with that behind the outline – so the outline will always be easily visible.

The CSS specifications leave the precise treatment of outlines to be determined by the browser but they do make suggestions as to how they may appear. Surprisingly, the truly unique suggestion is that an outline can be non-rectangular. This does not provide curved outlines (yet) but allows contiguous outlines to disappear, leaving a single non-rectangular outline around the content edges.

Suggested position at which to draw an outline, relative to the box model beneath, is just outside the border edge. The example opposite shows different treatment of the same outlines where padding of 5px has been added. The top screenshot shows the outlines positioned just outside the border of block-level and inline-level content boxes. In the bottom screenshot the border moves away from the heading content, while the outline remains in place, and contiguous sections of the outline around the inline span element content boxes have been collapsed to leave a single non-rectangular outline around the content.

outline.html

```
<h2>Gold Rush Fever</h2>
<p>By early 1849, gold fever was an epidemic.
<span>Farmers left their fields; merchants closed their
shops; soldiers left their posts - and made plans for
California.</span> Newspapers fanned the fires.</p>
```

outline.css

```
h2,p  { padding: 5px; width: 300px      }
h2    { border: 3px double blue;  background: aqua   }
p     { border: 3px dashed green; background: yellow }
/* set outlines... */
h2,span        { outline: 2px solid red   }
```

This example is illustrated with the Opera and Konqueror web browsers – the appearance may vary with Internet Explorer.

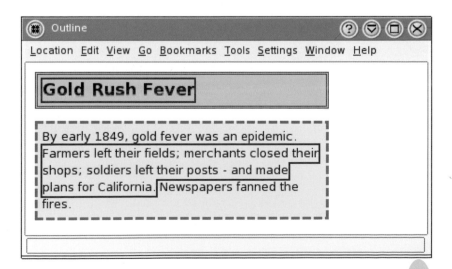

Summary

- The four CSS pseudo elements :before, :after, :first-line, and :first-letter can be included in a selector to generate content

- Both :before and :after pseudo elements use the content property to specify additional content – assigned as text strings within quotes, or as keywords open-quote, close-quote, or url()

- The attr() keyword can be used with the content property to specify an attribute whose value should be generated content

- A counter can be created by assigning a name and incremental value to the counter-increment property and can be reset by assigning its name and initial value to the counter-reset property

- The counter() property can recall the current value of a named counter specified within its parentheses

- Initial components of a block-level element can be styled with the :first-line and :first-letter pseudo elements

- Pseudo-classes :first-child and :lang() can be used to style content according to the document tree and language information

- The cursor property can specify a cursor by the keywords default, pointer, crosshair, move, text, wait, progress, help, n-resize, ne-resize, e-resize, se-resize, s-resize, sw-resize, w-resize, and nw-resize

- An image can be specified as a cursor by assigning its location to the cursor property using the url() keyword

- An outline can be created around, and above, content with the individual outline-style, outline-color, outline-width properties or with the shorthand outline property

- Assigning the invert keyword to the outline-color property automatically selects a color that ensures the outline is visible

Creating dynamic effects

This chapter demonstrates how CSS pseudo-classes can react to user-originated interface events by applying styles dynamically. Examples illustrate in-focus highlighting, rollover effects, slide-out tabs, drop-down menus, and responsive CSS "buttons".

Covers

Chapter Thirteen

Highlighting the current focus

Interactive components of an HTML document comprise those elements that can accept keyboard input, such as a text field, and those which can be activated by a user action, such as a push button or hyperlink. When one of these interactive components is selected by the user, typically by a mouse click or tab key, it is ready to be activated and is said to have "focus".

CSS provides the :focus pseudo-class which can be used to apply styling to the element that has current focus in a document – in recognition of the user's selection. The styling is removed from that element when the focus shifts to another element, as the user selects a different interactive component.

Focus only relates to interactive elements that can receive keyboard input, or be activated by the user somehow.

Highlighting the element in current focus is especially useful in lengthy forms with many input fields as it acts as a marker that easily identifies the progress through the form.

The example below has three interactive components – a text input, a submit button input, and a hyperlink. Initially no interactive component is in focus but any can be selected by the user, with a mouse click or using the tab key, to become in focus. The element with current focus is highlighted by the background color assigned to the style rule that targets that element:

focus.html

```
<form>
<fieldset>
<legend> Send for details </legend>
<label for = "addr">Enter your email address: </label>
<input id = "addr" type = "text">
<input type = "submit" value = "Send">
<a href = "http://samples">Samples Page</a>
</fieldset>
</form>
```

focus.css

```
/* set input focus highlights */
input:focus          { background: lime  }

/* set hyperlink focus highlights */
a:focus              { background: aqua  }
```

Focus

File   Edit   View   Favorites   Tools   Help

Send for details
Enter your email address: [   ] [Send]
Samples Page

Focus

File   Edit   View   Favorites   Tools   Help

Send for details
Enter your email address: [▓▓▓▓▓] [Send]
Samples Page

Focus

File   Edit   View   Favorites   Tools   Help

Send for details
Enter your email address: [   ] [Send]
Samples Page

Focus

File   Edit   View   Favorites   Tools   Help

Send for details
Enter your email address: [   ] [Send]
Samples Page

Styling hyperlinks by status

Hyperlinks in an HTML document appear in the color designated by the browsers default scheme to indicate their status as either "visited" or "unvisited". The status is determined by comparing the user's browser history and typically uses the Links colors from Internet Explorer's default scheme, as shown below:

![Colors dialog box with Colors section showing Text and Background options with Use Windows colors checkbox, and Links section showing Visited, Unvisited, Use hover color checkbox, and Hover options, with OK and Cancel buttons]

The CSS :link and :visited pseudo-classes can be used to assign different colors to indicate the history status of a target element.

Additionally, the :hover and :active pseudo-classes can be used to assign explicit colors to indicate the interactive status of a hyperlink. The color specified by the :hover pseudo-class is applied when the link has focus, ready to be activated, and that specified by the :active pseudo-class will be applied when the user actually activates the link, usually by clicking the mouse button.

Remember the difference between the pseudo-classes; Both :link and :visited apply static styles but :hover, :active, (and :focus) apply styles dynamically – in response to user actions.

It is important to recognize that the :link pseudo-class targets only those a anchor elements that include a href attribute, not fragment anchors which mark positions in the page.

In the example opposite the first style rule sets the color and font-weight for all anchor elements. Subsequent rules in the stylesheet explicitly specify non-default colors to indicate the status of the hyperlinks according to their history and interactive condition. The second hyperlink has already been activated to illustrate the application of the color indicating its "visited" status.

link-status.html

```
<ol>
<li><a name = "top">Fragment anchor</a>
<li><a href = "http://been-there">Visited link</a>
<li><a href = "http://go-there">Unvisited link</a>
</ol>
```

CSS

link-status.css

```
a            { color: blue; font-weight: bold }
a:link       { color: red    }   /* history status */
a:visited    { color: gray   }   /* history status */
a:hover      { color: green  }   /* interactive */
a:active     { color: orange }   /* interactive */
```

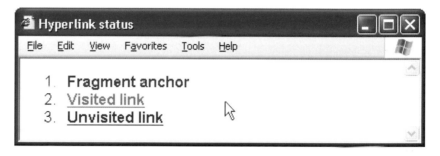

Reacting to interface events

User actions cause interface "events" to which the three dynamic CSS pseudo-classes, :focus, :hover and :active, can react. For instance, when a user clicks on a text input the Focus event occurs – to which the :focus pseudo-class can react by applying styles.

The :focus pseudo-class only relates to those elements that can receive input – but the :hover class relates to ANY element.

Perhaps more interestingly, when the user moves the cursor onto any element the MouseOver event occurs to which the :hover pseudo-class can react by applying styles to the target element. These are removed when the cursor moves off the element (as the MouseOut event occurs) creating a dynamic "rollover" effect.

Typically the rollover will highlight the target element by changing its content color or background color to become more prominent. Equally, the rollover might specify a different background image to create an image-swap – but this may not work too well on slower connections that need to wait for the new image to download.

A better image-swap alternative is to combine the images for both states into a single image file, then have the rollover reveal the appropriate half by specifying a different background position.

footprints.gif
size: 150x100 pixels
background: transparent

For instance, this example uses a combined image file that measures 150 pixels wide and 100 pixels high. It is specified as the background image to a div element that also measures 150 pixels wide but is only 50 pixels high – half that of the image height. The background image is positioned in the top left corner of the div element (0px 0px) so only the top half of the image is visible. Its position gets changed by the rollover, moving up by 50 pixels beyond the top left corner of the div element (0px -50px), so only the bottom half of the image is visible – a fast image-swap.

The HTML document simply lists the two empty div tags whose size and background are styled by rules in the stylesheet. An initial background color is applied to each one but changed in reaction to the MouseOver event to demonstrate a simple rollover effect:

```
<div id = "div-1"></div>

<div id = "div-2"></div>
```

rollover.html

rollover.css

```css
/* set divs size */
#div-1,#div-2          { width: 150px; height: 50px          }

/* set div-1 background colors */
#div-1                 { background-color: blue               }
#div-1:hover           { background-color: red                }

/* set div-2 background image, position, and colors */
#div-2                 {
background: url("footprints.gif") 0px 0px aqua                }

#div-2:hover           {
background: url("footprints.gif") 0px -50px lime              }
```

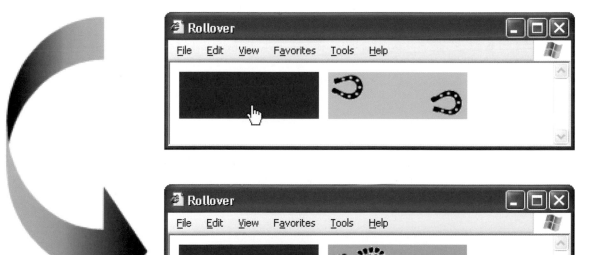

Interacting with CSS buttons

A rollover effect, as described in the previous example, can be combined with a hyperlink to create an interactive "button" using dynamic pseudo-classes to style anchor elements.

It is generally desirable to nest the anchor element within an outer element, of defined size, then apply a display:block style to the anchor so it expands up to the boundaries of its container. This means that the entire area of the containing element is "clickable" and the anchor element's background will fill the container.

In the following example the button container elements are provided by the dt elements of a definition list (chosen because a definition list does not supply item markers, unlike other list types). Individual rules specify the background color and border appearance of each anchor element according to its "state". When the MouseOver event occurs the :hover pseudo-class provides the rollover effect. Additionally, when the user then clicks on the hyperlink the MouseDown event occurs and the :active pseudo-class applies a further change of appearance to the "button":

buttons.css

Applying a display:block rule to the anchor elements is vital to the success of this effect.

```css
/* set button menu position */
dl#menu       { position: absolute;
                top: 10px; left: 20px; width: 150px      }

/* set general button styles */
dt.btn        { margin-bottom: 5px; text-align: center }

/* set general anchor styles - fill the container */
dt.btn a      { display: block; text-decoration: none;
                color: white; font-weight: bold         }

/* MouseOut state (default) */
dt.btn a             { background: blue;
                       border: 5px outset blue           }

/* MouseOver state (hover) */
dt.btn a:hover       { background: red;
                       border: 5px outset red            }

/* MouseDown state (active) */
dt.btn a:active      { background: green;
                       border: 5px inset green           }
```

```
<dl id = "menu">
<dt class = "btn"><a href = "a.html">Button 1</a></dt>
<dt class = "btn"><a href = "b.html">Button 2</a></dt>
<dt class = "btn"><a href = "c.html">Button 3</a></dt>
</dl>
```

buttons.html

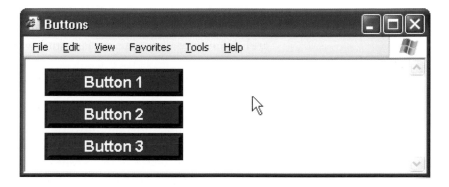

Moving within the document

In addition to changing the appearance of the target element, to create a rollover effect, the three dynamic CSS pseudo-classes :focus, :hover, and :active can apply styles that change the size or position of the target element to create a further dynamic effect. For instance, with absolutely positioned elements the style could specify different offset values to reposition the element.

Use dynamic repositioning with caution – it can hide other content and be unsettling for the user.

Alternatively the element size can be dynamically changed by specifying different values to its **padding** property. This is often a better option and is used in the example below to create dropdown tabs in a simple menu.

This example builds on the previous one by including the rollover effects and adding dynamic movement. Each tab is created as a list item in a **dt** element, but displayed horizontally by the **display:block** rule. When the MouseOver event occurs the **:hover** pseudo-class applies a **20px** value to the element's **padding-top** property – extending the tab downwards. This value is maintained by the **:active** pseudo-class when the tab is clicked, but it is removed when the MouseOut event returns it to the default state:

tabs.css

```
/* set tabs menu position */
dl#menu { position: absolute; top: 0px; left: 10px    }

/* set general tab styles - horizontal format */
dt.tab   { display: block; float: left;
           margin-right: 5px; text-align: center       }

/* set general anchor styles - fill the container */
dt.tab a    { display: block; text-decoration: none;
           color: white; font-weight: bold; width: 100px }

/* MouseOut state (default) */
dt.tab a { background: blue; border: 5px outset blue }

/* MouseOver state (hover) */
dt.tab a:hover { padding-top: 20px; background: red;
                 border-color: red                    }

/* MouseDown state (active) */
dt.tab a:active { padding-top: 20px; background: green;
                  border-color: green                 }
```

```
<dl id = "menu">
<dt class = "tab"><a href = "aa.html">Tab 1</a></dt>
<dt class = "tab"><a href = "bb.html">Tab 2</a></dt>
<dt class = "tab"><a href = "cc.html">Tab 3</a></dt>
</dl>
```

tabs.html

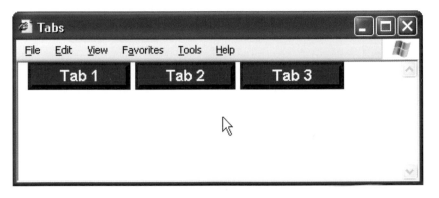

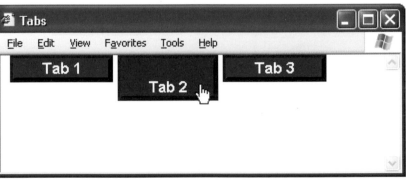

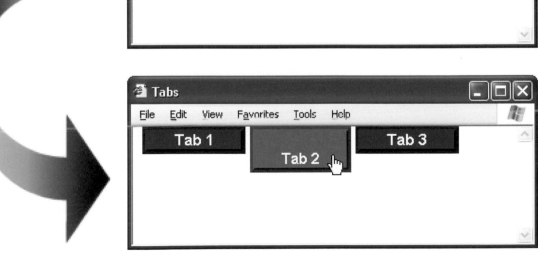

Hiding and revealing components

Besides the ability to style an element's appearance, position, and size, the three dynamic CSS pseudo-classes :focus, :active, and :hover can be used to control whether the element is even visible.

Specifying the hidden keyword to an element's visibility property will hide the element. Conversely it can be explicitly revealed by specifying the visible keyword to its visibility property.

Hidden elements still occupy space in the document – they just can't be seen.

In the following example each hyperlink in the list contains two image elements. The second image element in each link is assigned a common class attribute value so they may all be targeted by a single style rule. This specifies a common absolute position and sets their visibility value to hidden so they cannot be seen.

A further style rule uses the :hover pseudo-class to make the hidden second image within each hyperlink be visible when the user places the cursor over the first image within that link. Moving the cursor off the hyperlink hides the second image once more:

gallery.html

```html
<dl id = "pix">
<dt><a href="#"><img src = "thumb-1.jpg">
    <img class = "hid" src="pic-1.jpg"></a></dt>
<dt><a href="#"><img src = "thumb-2.jpg">
    <img class = "hid" src="pic-2.jpg"></a></dt>
<dt><a href="#"><img src = "thumb-3.jpg">
    <img class = "hid" src="pic-3.jpg"></a></dt>
</dl>
```

gallery.css

```css
/* set general thumbnail styles */
#pix { position: absolute; top: 0px; left: 0px    }
dt   { margin: 10px                                }
img  { border: none                                }

/* MouseOut state (default) - hide larger pictures */
#pix a img.hid {
    width: 250px; height: 150px;
    position: absolute; top: 10px; left: 120px;
    visibility: hidden                             }

/* MouseOver state (hover)- reveal larger picture */
#pix a:hover           { background: white        }
#pix a:hover img.hid   { visibility: visible      }
```

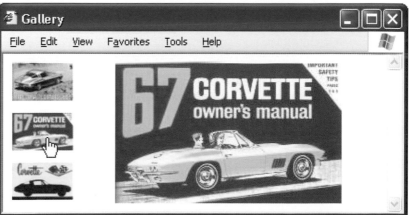

Summary

- The :focus pseudo-class can dynamically style elements that accept keyboard input and those which can be activated by the user

- Hyperlink status can be either "visited" or "unvisited"

- The :visited pseudo-class can specify static styles for those hyperlinks that are recorded in the browser history as "visited"

- Conversely, the :link pseudo-class can specify static styles for "unvisited" links – for anchor elements that have an href attribute

- The :hover pseudo-class can specify dynamic styles for the hyperlink in current focus, and the :active pseudo-class can specify dynamic styles for hyperlinks that are currently being activated

- The three dynamic pseudo-classes are :focus, :hover, and :active

- The :hover pseudo-class can create a "rollover" effect by dynamically changing the appearance of the target element – in reaction to the MouseOver interface event

- Additionally, the :active pseudo-class can indicate when an element is being activated by dynamically changing the appearance of the target element – in reaction to the MouseDown interface event

- Styles that have been dynamically applied to a target element by the :hover pseudo-class are automatically removed when the focus moves away – in reaction to the MouseOut interface event

- An element's size and position can be changed by dynamically specifying new values to its absolute coordinates or to its box model properties such as padding and margin

- An element's visibility property can be dynamically assigned the keywords hidden or visible to determine whether it can be seen

Reference section

This appendix provides a handy reference listing all the visual CSS properties and their possible values. It also includes useful at-a-glance guides describing each CSS selector, pseudo-class, and pseudo-element, with syntax reference and example rules.

Covers

Appendix

Properties and values

The tables in this section list by Name each visual CSS property and each possible Value.

Each CSS property can be applied to any HTML element unless specific target elements are given in the table. For instance, a border-collapse property can only be applied to table and inline-table elements, whereas a background property can be applied to any element.

Similarly, properties are not inherited unless specifically marked as "^ Inherited". For instance, the border-collapse property is inherited but the background property is not.

In each case the Initial Value is the default value that will be inferred unless a valid alternative value is explicitly specified in a style rule.

Name	Values	Initial Value
background	[*background-color* || *background-image* || *background-repeat* || *background-attachment* || *background-position*] | inherit	see individual properties
background-attachment	scroll | fixed | inherit	scroll
background-color	*color* | transparent | inherit	transparent
background-image	*url* | none | inherit	none
background-position	[[*length* | *percentage* | left | center | right] | [*length* | *percentage* | top | center | bottom] | [left | center | right] || [top | center | bottom]] | inherit	0% 0%
background-repeat	repeat | repeat-x | repeat-y | no-repeat | inherit	repeat
border-collapse (applies to table and inline-table elements)	collapse | separate | inherit ^Inherited	separate
border-spacing (applies to table and inline-table elements)	*length length* ? | inherit ^Inherited	0

Name	Values	Initial Value
border	[*border-width* || *border-style* || *border-color*] | inherit	see individual properties
border-top border-right border-bottom border-left	[*border-width* || *border-style* || *border-color*] | inherit	see individual properties
border-color	[*color* | transparent] { 1, 4 } | inherit	see individual properties
border-top-color border-right-color border-bottom-color border-left-color	*color* | transparent | inherit	the *color* value of that element
border-style	[none | hidden | dotted | dashed | solid | double | groove | ridge | inset | outset |] { 1, 4 } | inherit	see individual properties
border-top-style border-right-style border-bottom-style border-left-style	[none | hidden | dotted | dashed | solid | double | groove | ridge | inset | outset |] | inherit	none
border-width	[thin | medium | thick | *length*] { 1, 4 } | inherit	see individual properties
border-top-width border-right-width border-bottom-width border-left-width	thin | medium | thick | *length* | inherit	medium
bottom (applies to positioned elements}	*length* | *percentage* | auto | inherit	auto
caption-side (applies to table caption elements)	top | bottom | inherit ^Inherited	top
clear (applies to block-level elements)	left | right | both | none | inherit	none

Name	Values	Initial Value
clip (applies to absolutely positioned elements)	rect(*top* , *right* , *bottom* , *left*)	auto	inherit	auto
color	*color*	inherit ^Inherited	specified by user-agent
content (applies to :before and :after pseudo elements)	[*string*	*url*	*counter*	attr(*identifier*)	 open-quote	close-quote	no-open-quote	 no-close-quote]+	normal	inherit	normal
counter-increment	[*identifier integer* ?]+	none	inherit	none
counter-reset	[*identifier integer* ?]+	none	inherit	none
cursor	[[*url* ,]*	auto	default	pointer	crosshair	 move	e-resize	w-resize	 n-resize	ne-resize	nw-resize	 s-resize	se-resize	sw-resize	 text	wait	help	progress]	inherit ^Inherited	auto
direction	ltr	rtl	inherit ^Inherited	ltr
display	none	inline	block	inline-block	list-item	 run-in	table	inline-table	table-row-group	 table-header-group	table-footer-group	 table-row	table-column-group	table-column	 table-cell	table-caption	inherit	inline
empty-cells (applies to table-cell elements)	show	hide	inherit ^Inherited	show
float	left	right	none	inherit	none

Name	Values	Initial Value
font (may include optional values marked ?)	[[*font-style*		*font-variant*		*font-weight*] ? *font-size* [/ *line-height*] ?	*font-family*]	caption	icon	menu	message-box	small-caption	status-bar	inherit ^Inherited	see individual properties
font-family (may include optional values marked ?)	[[*family-name*	*generic-family*] ,] ? [*family-name*	*generic-family*]	inherit ^Inherited	specified by user-agent
font-size	xx-small	x-small	small	medium	large	x-large	xx-large	smaller	larger	*length*	*percentage*	inherit ^Inherited	medium
font-style	italic	oblique	normal	inherit ^Inherited	normal
font-variant	small-caps	normal	inherit ^Inherited	normal
font-weight	normal	bold	bolder	lighter	inherit	100	200	300	400	500	600	700	800	900 ^Inherited	normal
height (applies to block-level and replaced elements)	*length*	*percentage*	auto	inherit	auto
left (applies to positioned elements)	*length*	*percentage*	auto	inherit	auto
letter-spacing	*length*	normal	inherit ^Inherited	normal
line-height	*length*	*percentage*	*number*	normal	inherit ^Inherited	normal

Name	Values	Initial Value
list-style (applies to elements whose display property has a list-item value)	[*list-style-type* || *list-style-image* || *list-style-position*] | inherit ^Inherited	see individual properties
list-style-image (applies to elements whose display property has a list-item value)	*url* | none | inherit ^Inherited	none
list-style-position (applies to elements whose display property has a list-item value)	inside | outside | inherit ^Inherited	outside
list-style-type (applies to elements whose display property has a list-item value)	disc | circle | square | decimal | decimal-leading-zero | lower-roman | upper-roman | lower-greek | lower-latin | upper-latin | armenian | georgian | none | inherit ^Inherited	disc
margin	[*length* | *percentage* | auto] { 1, 4 } | inherit	see individual properties
margin-top **margin-right** **margin-bottom** **margin-left**	*length* | *percentage* | auto | inherit	0
max-height **max-width** (applies to all elements except inline non-replaced elements and table elements)	*length* | *percentage* | none | inherit	none
min-height **min-width** (applies to all elements except inline non-replaced elements and table elements)	*length* | *percentage* | inherit	0

Name	Values	Initial Value
outline	[*outline-color* || *outline-style* || *outline-width*] | inherit	see individual properties
outline-color	*color* | invert | inherit	invert
outline-style	none | dotted | dashed | solid | double | groove | ridge | inset | outset | inherit	none
outline-width	thin | medium | thick | *length* | inherit	medium
overflow (applies to block-level and replaced elements)	visible | hidden | scroll | auto | inherit	visible
padding	[*length* | *percentage*] { 1, 4 } | inherit	see individual properties
padding-top padding-right padding-bottom padding-left	*length* | *percentage* | inherit	0
position	static | relative | absolute | fixed | inherit	static
quotes	[*string string*]+ | none | inherit ^Inherited	specified by user-agent
right (applies to positioned elements)	*length* | *percentage* | auto | inherit	auto
table-layout (applies to table and inline-table elements)	auto | fixed | inherit	auto
text-align (applies to block-level elements)	left | center | right | justify | inherit ^Inherited	specified by user-agent
text-decoration	[underline || overline || line-through || blink] | none | inherit	none

Name	Values	Initial Value
text-indent (applies to block-level elements)	*length* | *percentage* | inherit ^Inherited	0
text-transform	uppercase | lowercase | capitalize | none | inherit ^Inherited	none
top (applies to positioned elements)	*length* | *percentage* | auto | inherit	auto
unicode-bidi	normal | embed | bidi-override | inherit	normal
vertical-align (applies to inline elements and table cells)	baseline | sub | super | top | middle | bottom | text-top | text-bottom | *length* | *percentage* | inherit	baseline
visibility	visible | hidden | collapse | inherit ^Inherited	inherit
white-space	normal | nowrap | pre | pre-wrap | pre-line | inherit ^Inherited	normal
width (applies to block-level and replaced elements)	*length* | *percentage* | auto | inherit	auto
word-spacing	normal | *length* | inherit ^Inherited	normal
z-index (applies to positioned elements)	auto | *integer* | inherit	auto

Selectors

The following tables in this section provide a brief description of each type of CSS selector together with its syntax pattern and an example style rule using that selector:

Universal selector	
Matches any element in the HTML document. If a rule has no explicit selector the universal selector is inferred	
Pattern:	*
Example: Target all elements	* { color: green }

Element selector	
Matches the specified named element in the HTML document. Every instance of the named element is matched	
Pattern:	element
Example: Target all p paragraph elements	p { color: green }

Descendant selector	
Matches a specified element that is a descendant of another specified element. The matched element can be of any descendant level – child, grandchild, great-grandchild, etc.	
Pattern:	element descendant-element
Example: Target all li list item elements of both ordered and unordered lists contained within any div element (child descendants of ol and ul elements – grandchildren of div)	div li { color: green }

Child selector

Matches a specified element that is a child of another specified element. This is more precise than the descendant selector as it only matches direct child elements — not other descendant levels

Pattern:	element > child-element
Example: Target each p paragraph element that is a direct child of a div element	div > p { color: green }

Adjacent sibling selector

Matches an element that immediately follows a specified sibling element in the document tree relationship

Pattern:	element + sibling-element
Example: Target each p paragraph element that immediately follows any h3 element	h3 + p { color: green }

Class selector

Matches the name assigned to a "class" attribute of an HTML element using dot notation to select that element

Pattern:	element.class-name
Example: Target each p paragragh element with a class attribute value of "grn"	p.grn { color: green }

ID selector

Matches the name assigned to an "id" attribute of an HTML element using hash notation to select that element

Pattern:	element#id-name
Example: Target each p paragraph element with an id attribute value of "grn"	p#grn { color: green }

Attribute selector	
Matches any element that includes the specified attribute	
Pattern:	element[attribute]
Example: Target each a anchor element that has an href attribute – regardless of its value	a[href] { color: green }

Attribute value selector	
Matches the exact value assigned to a specified attribute to select that element	
Pattern:	element[attribute = "value"]
Example: Target each a element with an exact href attribute value of "home"	a[href = "home"] { color: green }

Listed attribute value selector	
Matches the exact value from a space-separated list of values assigned to a specified attribute to select that element	
Pattern:	element[attribute ~= "value"]
Example: Target each span element which includes a class attribute value "grn"	span[class ~= "grn"] { color: green }

Partial attribute value selector	
Matches the first-part of a hyphenated value assigned to a specified attribute to select that element	
Pattern:	element[attribute |= "value"]
Example: Target each span element containing a hyphenated lang attribute value beginning with "es"	span[lang |= "es"] { color: green }

Pseudo-classes

The following tables in this section list each CSS pseudo-class together with a description of its application and an example style rule using that pseudo-class:

:lang	
Applies to an element based on the human language encoding as defined in the document header or by a lang attribute value. Works like the |= partial attribute value selector matching both single and hyphenated language identifiers (like "es" and "es-mx")	
Example: Target each span element defined as Spanish language encoding	span:lang(es) { color: green }

:first-child	
Applies to an element that is the first child of another element in the document tree relationship – the specified element is itself the target, not the first child of that element	
Example: Target each span element that is itself the first child of an outer containing element	span:first-child { color: green }

:focus	
Applies to an element during the time when it has the interface focus to accept keyboard events. Easiest recognized when an HTML form input box is displaying the text-input cursor – ready for the user to input text	
Example: Target each input element when it has the interface focus ready to receive text input	input:focus { background: lime }

:link
Applies to a hyperlink that <u>is not</u> known to have been visited according to the user agents history – the "link" state is mutually exclusive with the "visited" state described in the next table

Example: Target each a anchor element with an unvisited hyperlink	a:link { color: green }

:visited
Applies to a hyperlink that <u>is</u> known to have been visited according to the user agents history – the "visited" state is mutually exclusive with the "link" state described in the last table

Example: Target each a anchor element with a visited hyperlink	a:visited { color: red }

:hover
Applies to an element during the time when it is designated without being activated – hovering the mouse pointer within its boundaries to fire the "mouseover" interface event

Example: Target each span element when it is designated by the mouse pointer hovering over it	span:hover { background: lime }

:active
Applies to an element during the time when it is activated – clicking the mouse button within its boundaries to fire the "mousedown" interface event

Example: Target each span element when it is activated by the mouse button clicking on it	span:active { background: red }

Pseudo-elements

The following tables in this section list each CSS pseudo-element together with a description of what it generates and an example style rule using that pseudo-element:

:before	
Generates a pseudo-element to insert content before all other content in the specified element	
Example: Target each p paragraph and insert an opening square bracket before other content	p:before { content: "[" }

:after	
Generates a pseudo-element to insert content after all other content in the specified element	
Example: Target each p paragraph and insert an closing square bracket after other content	p:after { content: "]" }

:first-letter	
Generates a pseudo-element to style the very first letter of text contained within a specified element	
Example: Target the first letter within each p paragraph element	p:first-letter { font-size: larger }

:first-line	
Generates a pseudo-element to style the very first line of text contained within a specified element	
Example: Target the first line of text in each p paragraph element	p:first-line { color: green }

Index

D

F

H

height property 89, 109, 177
help keyword 154, 176
hexadecimal color notation 48
hidden keyword 92, 118, 156, 170, 175, 179, 180
hide keyword 126, 176
hover. *See* pseudo-class
HTML
    a element 162
    body element 30
    class attribute 24
    h3 element 30
    href attribute 162
    html element 30
    id attribute 25
    lang attribute 26
    link element 12
    p element 30
    src attribute 26
    style attribute 15
    ul element 30
hyperlink 162

I

icon keyword 177
identity selector # 25, 182
image-swap 164
image marker 136
important rules 35
importing external style sheets 14
import directive @ 14
inch units 50
indenting text 74
Inheritance 42
inherit keyword 174–180
inline-block keyword 89, 176
inline-level elements 84
inline-table keyword 176
inline content box 84
inline keyword 176
inline style rules 15
inset keyword 92, 175, 179
inside keyword 137, 178
interactive button 166
interface event 164
invert keyword 156, 179
italic keyword 64, 177

J

justify keyword 70, 179

L

lang. *See* pseudo-class
large/larger keyword 60, 177
left keyword 116, 142, 174–176, 179
left property 108, 177
letter-spacing property 74, 177
lighter keyword 62, 177
line-height property 72, 177
line-through keyword 76, 179
line box 72
link. *See* pseudo-class
list-item keyword 176
list-style-image property 136, 178
list-style-position property 137, 178
list-style-type property 134, 146, 178
list-style property 178
list-style shorthand property 138
listed attribute value selector 183
list marker 134
lower-greek keyword 134, 178
lower-latin keyword 134, 178
lower-roman keyword 134, 178
lowercase keyword 76, 180
ltr keyword 78, 176

M

margin-bottom property 102, 178
margin-left property 102, 178
margin-right property 102, 178
margin-top property 102, 178
margin area 82, 92
margin property 82, 100, 106, 178
margin shorthand 102
margin styles 100
marker 134
max-height property 178

N

O

P

Q

V

W

X

Z